D1592839

HIGH PLAINS PRESS

Dreamers & Schemers

Dreamers & Schemers

Profiles from
Carbon County, Wyoming's Past

Lori Van Pelt

HIGH PLAINS PRESS

FIRST PRINTING

10 9 8 7 6 5 4 3 2 1

Library of Congress Cataloging-in-Publication Data

Van Pelt, Lori
Dreamers and schemers : profiles from Carbon County,
Wyoming's past / by Lori Van Pelt.
p.   cm. -- (Dreamers and schemers series ; no.1)
Includes bibliographical references and index.
ISBN 0-931271-50-9 (acid-free paper).
ISBN 0-931271-49-5 (pbk. acid-free paper)
1. Pioneers--Wyoming--Carbon County--Biography.
2. Carbon County (Wyo.)--Biography.
3. Carbon County (Wyo)--History.
I. Title.
II. Series: Van Pelt, Lori, 1961–
Dreamers and schemers series ; no.1.
F832.C4V36   1999
978.7'86'020922--dc21
[B]   98-47689
CIP

HIGH PLAINS PRESS
539 CASSA ROAD
GLENDO, WYOMING 82213

DEDICATION

To everyone who's reached for a dream,

especially Eugene and Cid and their parents.

Foreword

READERS WHO RACE through books on Wyoming history often remember Carbon County simply as a political subdivision with extensive coal deposits in the south-central part of the state. Carbon County is that, of course, but a whole lot more. The history of Carbon County is the history of the American West in microcosm. It chronicles a heritage woven into the fabric of our nation.

If there is one persistent feature about Carbon County, it is diversity. Since December 1868, the county boundaries themselves have been redrawn several times to accommodate changing needs. Her natural resources and terrain also vary, from a High Plains grassland ecosystem, to semi-arid intermountain basins, to lush river valleys and rugged snow-capped mountains. Fluctuations in climate range from hot, dry summers to cold, snowy winters. And if you dislike the day's weather, wait a minute, it too will probably change. Even her history is dynamic, revealing every aspect of our evolving perspective on the western frontier.

For all that characterizes Carbon County, no attribute is more typical of her diversity than is the personal achievements of her residents. Her citizens contributed substantially to every traditional theme that defined the western frontier in North America at the close of the Victorian age. Euroamerican settlement, military activity, the livestock industry, mineral development, community service, politics, and pure adventure are all chapters in her colorful past.

The profiles of thirty-one personalities in this book offer snapshots of men and women whose behavior helped shape Carbon County. Some were good, law abiding citizens; a few were cold, ruthless outlaws. Some immigrants only achieved notoriety at the local level, while others left an indelible mark on the national scene. Their achievements are obvious to some, obscure to others, but relevant to all who want to learn more about this part of Wyoming.

The author, Lori Van Pelt, is a relative newcomer to Wyoming, but she is no tenderfoot. Her solid journalistic skills have helped her plant deep roots in the North Platte River valley. While her familiarity with the Saratoga and Encampment area is manifest throughout, she includes all corners of the county in this, her first book. Writers who prepare biographical glimpses into the past always struggle in choosing which pioneers to showcase and which to exclude. Ms. Van Pelt survived this ordeal and did an admirable job bringing together the sometimes conflicting primary and secondary source material to offer this collection of "dreamers and schemers" in Carbon County.

Open the book. Journey back in time to an earlier century, to Carbon County's youth. Meet some of the people who lived there as the first boundaries of the county were drawn. Taste the flavor of her dynamic, cultural heritage. You will know more about the region when you close the book than you did when you began.

Carbon County history grows on you. Be patient and attentive, you will learn to appreciate it. Carbon County offers some tough lesson at times, but they are ones that will endure beyond all challenges, all obstacles. Carbon County's historical legacy is the foundation of her continued existence.

MARK E. MILLER

WYOMING STATE ARCHEOLOGIST

Introduction

CARBON COUNTY'S HISTORY contains many fascinating people, some who are well-known for reasons good and bad, and some who never laid a claim to fame and probably would not prefer to have it now. Although this book features some of the people I found interesting, it certainly cannot hold them all.

I began working on this project to educate myself about Carbon County's history. A native Nebraskan, I've adopted Wyoming as my home state. The landscape of western Nebraska, with its rolling plains dotted with spiky yucca plants and limestone bluffs, contrasts sharply with the mountainous terrain and salty sagebrush flats of south-central Wyoming. The ruggedness of the landscape appeared to infuse the people's history. Stories I heard, tales passed around to tourists, left me eager to learn more. Lynchings and massacres figured prominently, interspersed among copper mine discoveries, medical miracles, the travails of trail travel, political achievements, and quieter events, like the movement of an artist's pen to record the era.

I discovered that I knew very little about the history and the people of the county where I reside. Few books chronicle the county's history. Those that do exist provide information on certain towns or events within the county's borders. For me, people bring history to life. Their lives show the heartaches and hopes condensed into facts buried in dusty stacks of papers.

Carbon County and its people began my quest into the past. I listened to stories, legends, rumors. To educate myself, I worked as a volunteer docent at the Saratoga Museum. I also visited the Grand Encampment Museum in Encampment, the Medicine Bow Museum in Medicine Bow, and the Carbon County Museum in Rawlins.

I searched in the Wyoming State Archives in Cheyenne and at the American Heritage Center in Laramie. I interviewed people living now who treasure the tales of their ancestors.

I wanted to learn how people lived in what is now known as Carbon County. What interested them? Why did they choose to live here, in an area oft-described as tough country?

Through reading and researching the lives of these people, I discovered not only a wealth of information about the county's history, but an abundance of stories, illustrating the optimism and strength of the human spirit.

This book features historical biographies of thirty-one people who left a mark on Carbon County. Many of them reached for what seemed unattainable, but through their perseverance and their belief in the bounty of the West, they struggled and achieved. For what dream, if the dreamer tried hard enough, was not attainable in the glorious West?

Some attained unbelievable success. Others harbored darker dreams, weaving their schemes in that wide-open time and place. Some became legends still cloaked in controversy. Others faded from the limelight quickly, perhaps appearing now only in the brown tints of old photographs.

With the limited scope of this book, it was impossible to include everyone of interest. These, then, are the stories I found particularly fascinating as I attempted to display a good cross-section of the county's history. The book begins with mountain man Jim Baker, who built the first permanent cabin in Wyoming in the Little Snake River Valley in 1873, and ends with Charles Winter, who at the turn of the century lived in Encampment but later became a Wyoming Representative to Congress when he resided in Natrona County. The people chosen for this work lived during a fifty-year time span from the 1860s into the early 1900s. For some, like Winter, Carbon County was a stepping stone. Others just passed through, and some lived here for the greater parts of their lives.

These are only some of the men and women who made Carbon County such an interesting place to live during the latter years of the nineteenth century. Their occupations run the gamut from ranchers to ruffians, from lawmen to outlaws, and from doctors to artists.

Each one had some stake in forming the county. Some left legacies that affect Carbon County still. Some of them, through their life choices, their hopes and dreams, ultimately influenced the direction of the State of Wyoming.

If you seek more in-depth information about Carbon County, Wyoming, especially the Saratoga and Encampment area, I recommend reading local historian Gay Day Alcorn's book, *Tough Country.* Visiting the local museums, as well as researching at the Wyoming State Archives in Cheyenne and the American Heritage Center at the University of Wyoming in Laramie, helped draw a vivid picture of the past for me and might shed light on your own questions about the people I've selected and others who lived in this area during the designated time period.

Their successes and courage inspire me. I hope you will find encouragement to reach for your dreams as you read these pages, too.

Table of Contents

❧✦❧

"[Jim Baker's] home is the mountains and his companions Indians and wild animals."

From the article, "A Frontier Character,"
in the Cheyenne Daily Leader, January 17, 1877

❧✦❧

"An account of [Baker's] hair breadth escapes from Mexicans and Indians would fill a large book, and although covered with scars from wounds received while a trader, yet he is now at an advanced age and more robust than many men at 25."

From an article published on September 5, 1872,
in the (Pueblo) Colorado Chieftain and quoted in the book,
The Mountain Men and the Fur Trade of the Far West,
edited by LeRoy R. Hafen

Jim Baker

AN 1877 ISSUE OF the *Cheyenne Daily Leader* called Jim Baker "a frontier character." The article stated that Baker was as "gnarled and grizzled as one of the many old pines that have graced the mountain peaks."

At the time, Baker was nearly sixty years old and had survived battles with Indians as well as battles with nature. He loved the outdoors and displayed a strong independent streak. Baker had spent nearly forty years trapping, hunting, and serving as a government scout in the American West, largely in the area that would become Wyoming.

The article stated, "It would be a worse punishment for him to be compelled to live in a civilized country than the State Prison for most men."

But the man from Illinois who would become a legendary mountain man, trapper, and Indian fighter was a little nervous on his first trip to the Rockies in 1838. In Nolie Mumey's book on Baker's life, she writes that Baker depended upon Jim Bridger's guidance as he traveled with a group of trappers on his first trip through Indian lands. Though the men were stopped and examined by resentful Indians several times while crossing the Laramie Plains, Bridger's ability to deal with Indians helped the group safely reach their destination.

But that nervousness about Indian encounters dissipated quickly, and Baker went on not only to fight Indians, but eventually to live among them and marry Indian women. The *Leader* stated, however, that "his warmest friend and inseparable companion" was his rifle.

He was not known for using his rifle unwisely when he was sober. However, Mumey states that "when drunk he became very violent, boisterous, and frequently very dangerous." In spite of this, his reputation was that of a kind, loving man. John Steele wrote in *Across the Plains in 1850*, "Bigotry or avarice found no place in his heart; the jarring interests of society were unheard."

🐾🐾🐾

Born in 1818 in Belleville, Illinois, Jim Baker spent his childhood years in Springfield. He received little formal education, but he enjoyed the outdoors. At the age of twenty, Baker walked to St. Louis, where he first met Jim Bridger. Bridger was recruiting men for the American Fur Company. Baker signed on for eighteen months.

Baker spent the winter of 1838 and all of 1839 hunting and trapping on the Green River and in the Wind River Mountains, in present-day Wyoming. When his term with the fur company expired, he returned to Illinois.

But it wasn't the same anymore. Trapping and hunting had gotten into his blood. He remained in Illinois until the spring of 1841. In that year, he experienced what may have been his most memorable exploit in what is now Carbon County. He was asked to search for Henry Fraeb, a trapper friend of Jim Bridger's, along the Little Snake River. Fraeb was feared to be held by hostile Indians.

It was Baker's second trip to the Rockies, a journey he began alone. He briefly joined a group traveling west, but soon traveled alone again. He traveled down the Green River Valley by himself, a dangerous journey for a white man because of Indian unrest.

Baker arrived at his destination and joined Jim Bridger's camp which was then at Henry's Fork of the Green River (the camp was later moved to what is now called Battle Creek). He was relieved to learn that Fraeb was safe and camped with other trappers near the Little Snake River.

On August 21, 1841, Baker and another man were hunting across the Little Snake River from Fraeb's camp. Spotting a cloud of dust in the mountains, they ran for the camp, where they soon became embroiled in a two-day battle with Indians identified as Sioux, Cheyenne, and Arapaho.

Jim Baker. This photo is believed to have been taken by M.D. Houghton about 1879. (Courtesy Wyoming Division of Cultural Resources)

Fraeb was one of the first men killed, and Baker took charge. The bloody battle killed most of the trappers' horses, and claimed one hundred Indians. A young Arapaho woman leading the warriors did not retreat until her own horse had been shot.

The trappers fared better; only four were killed in the fracas which earned the town of Battle its name. The trappers, with only one round of gunpowder left, traveled on to Bridger's Camp on the Green River.

Though nothing remains of Battle now, travelers along Wyoming Highway 70 can drive over Battle Pass and stop to admire Battle Lake.

☙❦❧

Historian Mumey reported that the winters of 1845 and 1846 in southern Wyoming were hard; most of the horses and wild game froze to death. Baker, traveling with a band of trappers above Saratoga, Wyoming, decided to travel to Utah to join another group of trappers. The trappers rustled about four thousand horses from Mexicans and Spaniards in southern California.

By 1846, Baker had become friendly with Shoshone and Bannock Indians, tribes who were amicable to white men at the time. He participated in hunting expeditions with the Indians and was soon living with the tribe. He adopted their customs and culture, including beliefs in their superstitions and the cures of their medicine men.

Baker's life with the Indians included romance rivaling the stories told in the most adventurous romance novels. Mumey told of two of Baker's romances with Indian women, each with its own brand of adventure and excitement.

One romance developed when a tribe of Blackfeet Indians raided the Shoshone village where Baker lived and kidnapped the chief's daughter, Marina. Baker and another Indian rode on a successful rescue mission, and Baker earned the privilege of returning Marina to her father. He was often invited to the chief's lodge afterward.

Romance blossomed between Baker and Marina, who were married in October 1847 on the banks of the Seeds-ke-dee-Agie or Green River. According to Mumey, during the ceremony Baker wore hunter's clothes—beaver cap, leggings, a buckskin coat, and Indian moccasins. Marina made him a necklace from the claws of a grizzly bear Baker had killed on the Wind River Range, an emblem of bravery.

❧❧❧

Baker operated a ferry and a store along the Green River in the late 1840s and early 1850s. In an interview in the *Denver Republican* in 1893, as an old man, Baker recalled that he charged ten dollars a wagon to ferry travelers across the Green River which was less than seventy-five feet wide. Prices were high at the time. A shotgun cost forty dollars and a rifle one hundred dollars. Blankets were fifteen dollars and calico shirts cost five dollars.

He didn't stay in the ferry business very long, however. He soon became a government scout. Baker became an explorer and a guide, leading parties through the Rockies. He fought Indians from various tribes, including Crows, Sioux, Apaches, and Utes.

In 1852, Kit Carson invited Baker to accompany him on a trapping expedition in September. Baker traveled to Rayado, New Mexico, where Carson lived, and joined the party which included Jim Bridger.

During this expedition, the trappers made a large loop starting on the Arkansas River and progressively trapping along the South Platte, North Platte, Sweetwater, Wind River, and wintering on the Green River. Then, with spring weather, they moved to the Little Snake, Yampa and Grand Rivers, completing their loop back on the Arkansas River.

After the successful trip, with a good stock of furs, the trappers remained at Carson's ranch in Rayado for two weeks. According to Mumey, it was the last time the trappers assembled together.

Baker returned home to discover terrible sadness. His wife, Marina, had died.

But Baker was destined to find love again—this time with a young Sioux woman named Flying Fawn. Their love story included another daring rescue; but this time, from the forces of nature. And this time, a jealous suitor figured in the plot. Another Indian, Flash of Fire, loved Flying Fawn, too.

Baker rescued Flying Fawn; her father, Long Lance; and Flash of Fire, her cousin, from a raging blizzard. The Sioux Indians had been traveling to the Grand Encampment rendezvous, which was held in the early 1850s.

The Grand Encampment was located at the site of the present-day town of Encampment, Wyoming, not far from Battle Pass. Trappers gathered from across the country to meet agents who purchased their furs.

A late-April blizzard created snowdrifts from five to fifteen feet deep. Another trapper, Jean Laborde, had learned from an Indian messenger that the Indians were staying twenty miles down the river, but they had no provisions. Baker organized the rescue party, and it wasn't long before he fell in love with Flying Fawn.

Flash of Fire had other ideas. He hid, ready to shoot arrows at Baker as he and Flying Fawn stood before her father, anxious to be married.

Long Lance, aware of Flash of Fire's jealousy, killed his nephew with a single arrow before Baker even became aware of the danger. It is not known if Baker actually married Flying Fawn. Her name does not emerge in research again.

Information on Baker's family life is sketchy and conflicting. Leighton Baker wrote that Baker eventually fathered fourteen children by three wives. Marina bore sons William and Joseph and daughter Jane. Second wife Mary bore her namesake Mary plus Isabel, Madeline, Nancy, Kate, Thomas, Buck, Jim, Liza and Elsie. Mary's sister Eliza bore Jennie. Sisters Mary and Eliza were also called Monkey and Beans.

Baker served as chief scout for General Harvey at Fort Laramie, and in 1857 during the "Mormon War," he led Captain Marcy's troops from Fort Bridger to Fort Union for provisions.

He settled in Colorado during the 1859 gold rush, proving up land under the Homestead Act. His Colorado home was located in the area that would grow into the city of Denver, and the ford at Clear Creek became known as Baker's Crossing. In 1859, spring run-off was high, and crossing the creek became dangerous. Baker built and operated a toll bridge to help people cross the creek.

Baker guided Ute Indian agent Daniel C. Oakes in the 1860s to the spot where the White River Agency would be located. Marshall Sprague, in his book *Massacre: The Tragedy at White River,* reported that Baker had two Snake Indian wives at the time, Monkey and Beans, who were sisters.

Baker scouted for a railroad survey party to Salt Lake in 1872, and then he returned to Wyoming Territory in 1873. He raised cattle, using the JB brand.

Baker again traveled to Colorado's White River Agency as a guide, but the second time proved more difficult. Colonel Wesley Merritt, leader of the Fifth United States Cavalry, selected Baker as his guide when he took relief forces there after the massacre of Major Thomas Thornburgh by Ute Indians during the Battle of Milk Creek.

❦❦❦

The *Denver Republican* of June 8, 1893, reported a visit Baker made to Denver. Baker was seventy-five at the time and had outlived nearly anyone who could contradict him. It stated, "Jim Baker is in town. Of course, everybody who knows anything about anybody knows at least something about Jim Baker, the old-time scout. When Jim Baker comes to town it is something like the blooming of the century plant, and attracts far more attention."

The article called him the oldest living scout and said, "His life is a part of the history of the West, and it is one of the most interesting chapters." He was described as "tall, broad-shouldered, with light-colored hair allowed to hang to his shoulders, but never a gray streak in it, with a bright face" although his walk suggested great age.

Baker was then living on the Snake River, and the article reported that "the wilder the country the more to his tastes." He recalled being in Denver before it was much more than a prairie, guiding troops under Colonel Mesa, the father-in-law of General McClellan, to Fort Bridger to reinforce General Albert Sidney Johnson's army who were "looking after" the Mormons at the time.

Baker recalled in that interview that he and two other guides took General Johnson's 1857 expedition against the Mormons to Fort Bridger. Winter was approaching, and there was no feed for the horses and mules, who died. The guides were ordered to take men to New Mexico to acquire mules. Baker, unfamiliar with New Mexico, didn't guide the group again until they reached Cherry Creek on the return trip.

He discovered gold while guiding Colonel Mesa on the Cherry Creek Trail to Rawlins, he recalled in the article, and returned to the place where he'd found it. He wasn't a miner, he said, but a hunter, and the Utes cleaned out his mules.

"I said mining had no charms for me, nor has it, but I hauled into Denver the first load of stone coal that ever was taken out of the ground here," Baker said.

He said the railroad drove him out of Denver. He had been freighting with mules and making good money when "in came the Union Pacific and started hauling stuff for 2 cents a pound; so I went farther back, and I'm on Snake River now."

Baker traveled annually from his Wyoming ranch to Steamboat Springs, Colorado, to prospect, believing that huge mineral reserves were located there. He is honored in the Colorado Hall of Fame for his service as a pioneer scout and homesteader, but he disliked notoriety, and perhaps did not achieve the same amount of recognition as other trappers and scouts of the time because of it.

Mumey, in her sketch of Baker in the book *The Mountain Men*, stated, "Baker was as rugged as the mountains where he had spent most of his life. His wrinkled face and forehead contained lines chiseled by nature; his many adventures were clearly written on his bronzed features. Truly he was a man of the mountains." Considered "a man of outstanding qualities, loyal and trustworthy," Baker was described by Frank Hall, an early Colorado state official and historian as "kind-hearted, honest, and reliable."

Mumey stated, "Jim could speak several Indian dialects and his services were valuable to any expedition among the red men."

Baker built the first permanent cabin in Wyoming in 1873 in the Little Snake River Valley on the Wyoming-Colorado border. Baker's cabin, listed in the register of National Historic Places, stands on the Savery, Wyoming, museum grounds. Made of hand-hewn logs, it served as an early trading post. The two-story cabin was also home to Baker's family.

In 1917, the Wyoming Legislature voted to move Baker's cabin to Cheyenne, the state capital. The cabin was returned to the Little Snake River Museum and rededicated in 1977. It stands as a memorial to a man who had become a legend.

Baker died in his cabin on the Little Snake River on May 15, 1898.

Jim Baker's cabin, now at the Little Snake River Museum. (Author's photo)

Jim Baker is buried on a hill near the museum, in a family cemetery, which is still tended by a great-grandson of the legendary mountain man. The hill behind the cemetery, Baker's Peak, bears his name.

The marker on his grave contains this epitaph:

"One of the old Pioneers / of the Rocky Mountains / Contemporary of Kit Carson / Jim Bridger Fremont / And the Rest Who Helped / To Civilize this District / A Government Scout Guide / and Indian Fighter / His Memory Should be Respected / Forever by those who Live / In all this Region / The Fighting Land of the Indian Tribes."

A variety of portraits of Jim Baker adorn the inside walls of the entrance to the Little Snake River Museum, including a newly-created life-size painting of the man whose experiences seem larger than life.

Jim Baker earned his place in the history of the West through his achievements as a trapper, hunter, Indian fighter, and government scout. His eighty-year life, much of it spent fighting against and also living with Indians, was as colorful as his red hair. His hair, and his association with the Indians, earned him the nickname of the "red-haired Shoshone."

Carbon County was formed as one of the original five counties of Wyoming, carved from a part of Dakota Territory on July 25,1868. The original five counties of Wyoming Territory extended from the southern border to the northern border of the territory, and each county seat was on the Union Pacific Railroad.

Before Wyoming was created, the area that would become known as Carbon County had been part of the territories of Nebraska, Idaho, and Dakota.

Land that would become Carbon County was included in the Louisiana Purchase of 1803, the Mexican Cession of 1843, and the Texas Annexation of 1845.

In 1870, formal government formed in Carbon County, twenty years prior to Wyoming's statehood.

Information compiled from "Carbon County" by Margaret Baker
in *The Encyclopedia of Wyoming, Volume I,*
and from *Carbon County History,*
compliments of the Rawlins–Carbon County Chamber of Commerce

Ben Holladay

THE ROMANCE OF THE prairies, the quest for gold, the hope for a better life, and the promise of adventure called many people westward in the mid-1800s. Transportation methods included walking, riding a horse, and traveling by wagon. Those seeking luxury found a stagecoach more to their taste, especially if it was part of the Overland Stage Company line.

Ben Holladay—a man who loved a good joke, who had race-horses and cigars named for him, whose passion for gambling found release in the stock market—contributed to the opening of the west and Carbon County in an opulent and unforgettable manner.

Holladay's Overland Stage Company brought many people west and delivered mail through what was known in the early 1860s as Dakota Territory, overcoming obstacles such as bad weather and Indian attacks.

The Union and the Confederacy battled the Civil War as the emigrants traveling westward to California and Oregon battled against other foes. With federal troops involved in the Civil War, Indian difficulties escalated. Volunteers often protected travelers because there weren't enough soldiers along the route.

Author J. V. Frederick, in his book, *Ben Holladay, The Stagecoach King*, said, "To the isolated communities of the west [Holladay's] stagecoaches had brought letters, books, magazines, and congressional documents to strengthen the bonds of union with the east, at a time when disruption of communication might have resulted in disruption of the union. And he had patriotically maintained his lines of communications, carrying on under severe financial losses and against almost overwhelming obstacles, as befitted a true stagecoach king."

Holladay purchased the transportation firm of Russell, Majors, and Waddell in 1862 for $100,000. The route stretched from Atchinson, Kansas, to Salt Lake City. Russell, Majors, and Waddell Company, the largest overland transportation company in business in 1857, had won the contract to haul freight to Utah for Johnston's army. This began the era of large scale freighting along the Oregon Trail. The firm then expanded into stage and mail service and eventually organized the Pony Express.

According to Louise Bruning Erb in *The Bridger Pass Overland Trail 1862-1869*, the firm had been renamed the Central Overland California and Pike's Peak Express, but earned the nickname "Clean Out of Cash and Poor Pay" prior to Holladay's purchase of it.

Holladay operated the mail route on the northern Oregon Trail (via South Pass) for a few months and then moved it south, according to Erb. She wrote, "The increasing Indian depredations and Holladay's desire to serve the citizens of Denver City with freight, mail, and transportation, and also to save 150 miles distance, convinced him and the Postmaster General to change mail service and emigrant travel to the Bridger Pass route [Cherokee Trail] through southern Wyoming. This southern route had not had much Indian activity and was thought to be safer, but that would soon change."

The Cherokee Trail had been used by the Cherokee Indians during their 1849 trek to California. It was optimistically thought that the stages could average ten miles per hour on the new trail, renamed the Overland Trail.

Fort Halleck, named for Henry Halleck, was built in July of 1862 to protect the newly-named trail. The fort was built near the base of Elk Mountain between the North Platte River (later the site of Fort Fred Steele) and Rock Creek. The blacksmith shop, listed on the National Register of Historic Places, and a small cemetery still exist. These reminders of the past stand today on private property.

The area around Fort Halleck proved to be dangerous for travelers. Frederick stated in his book that during the summer of 1863, thirty-four mules were taken by Indians from the stage line at Fort Halleck and never recovered. The loss was estimated at $6,800.

Frederick also stated that Bob Spotswood, the superintendent of the Overland Stage line, hauled mail in an army ambulance from

Sulphur Springs Station to Fort Halleck on June 15, 1865. The next day, nearly one hundred Indians raided the Sulphur Springs Station.

Indians were active that summer between Virginia Dale (located on the present-day Wyoming-Colorado border) and Fort Halleck. Livestock was stolen, the Sage Creek Station was burned, and Holladay's company was forced to abandon many stagecoach stations along that route.

And though Wyoming had not yet been designated a territory, Ben Holladay's Overland Stage Company brought passengers through the area, hauled the mail, and helped bring civilization across the expanding United States. Other stagecoach stops in what would become Carbon County included Sulphur Springs, Medicine Bow, Elk Mountain Station, North Platte Crossing, Pass Creek, Pine Grove, Bridger's Pass, Washakie, and Duck Lane.

Holladay earned the nickname "The Stagecoach King" because he eventually controlled nearly five thousand miles of stage lines across the country.

🦋🦋🦋

Born in New York, Holladay moved from Kentucky to Missouri in 1837, remaining in Missouri until 1859. Possessed of the entrepreneurial spirit, Holladay and his brother Dave owned a packing plant, which later became a flour mill. In 1856, it became the Blue Springs distillery which made bourbon in Weston, Missouri. Holladay also traded with Indians in Kansas and, for a time, owned a hotel. With little schooling, Holladay's strength stood in his ability to manage men. He also possessed shrewd business sense.

Holladay had five brothers and one sister. His brother, Joseph, eventually became associated with Holladay's stagecoach business in Salt Lake City. Brother James helped Ben early in the stage business, before he moved to Colorado Territory. But Ben would be the only Holladay sibling to gain international fame.

In 1840, Ben Holladay eloped with Ann Calvert of Weston, Missouri. They had two daughters, Jennie and Pauline, and two sons, Benjamin and Joe.

As a young entrepreneur Holladay received the contract to freight supplies to troops fighting in the Mexican War in 1846. Freighting supplies from the Missouri River, Holladay earned profits as high as two hundred per cent. But Holladay did not spend his profits frivolously. He purchased government surplus mules, oxen, and wagons at low prices.

He began his own journey on the road to becoming one of the most famous men in transportation history.

By 1861, Holladay's enterprise contained four hundred coaches, five freight wagons, five thousand horses and mules and several thousand oxen.

Velma Linford, in her book *Wyoming, Frontier State*, called Holladay "a man of great business ability." Holladay was determined to make his stage and mail line the "greatest on the globe." He purchased only the best livestock, made improvements to the stations along the route, and required the best stagecoaches. Linford wrote, "Some of his Abbott-Downing stages were long enough to carry 12 or 15 passengers besides the express agent, the mails, and the driver. [Holladay] arranged with other companies to allow his passengers to buy through-tickets to the coast, although he did not own the entire line."

Frederick wrote that business came first for Ben Holladay, who was "irascible when crossed." He fired employees who drank too much and prohibited them from using profanity "offensively or promiscuously."

His drivers were loyal, though, and one of them became internationally famous in his own right. William F. (Buffalo Bill) Cody drove the stage between Plum Creek, Nebraska Territory, and Fort Kearny, also in Nebraska Territory. Cody also drove between Three Crossings and Split Rock in Dakota Territory. (Split Rock is a National Historic Site now in Natrona County, Wyoming, located only a few miles north of the present Carbon County border.)

Buffalo Bill used an incident that happened during his stage-coach-driving days for his Wild West Show. The show created a reenactment of the Sioux Indians' attack on the coach Buffalo Bill drove between Three Crossings and Split Rock. The division agent riding along was hit, but passengers fired back at the Indians and the stagecoach was rescued at Three Crossings.

Despite the obstacles in transporting passengers westward across the territories fraught with danger, and despite Holladay's vast business dealings, he was never associated with corruption. Holladay

Street in Denver was named for the businessman, but its name was later changed to Market Street to disassociate Holladay's good name from the bad reputation the area had gained.

Frederick stated that Holladay had a "dynamic and colorful personality." He enjoyed luxurious living and owned several "pretentious" homes until he retired from the stagecoach business. According to Frederick, "A friend once said that Ben wanted the halls of his Weston mansion big enough to drive a wagon through, and with this idea in mind all his homes must have been selected."

Along with the Weston home, Holladay owned homes in Washington, D.C., a brownstone mansion in New York, and a castle called Ophir Place in Westchester County, New York.

Holladay became a successful financier, and his mining interest in the Ophir Silver Mine in Nevada Territory gained him a minor fortune. At his eastern Ophir Place estate, he garnered another nickname, "the silver king."

Ophir Place was perhaps his most luxurious home. It stood on a thousand-acre tract at White Plains, New York, about sixty miles from New York City. A narrow-gauge railroad ran to the home, where a buffalo herd grazed in the park. The home cost an estimated one million dollars to build.

Holladay's Washington home was grand as well. His wife enjoyed entertaining, and the Washington home was purchased when Holladay earned the mail contract. It was advantageous for him to live in Washington. The President, members of Congress, and the postal department all had to approve payment on the mail contracts.

A classical library, oil paintings by fine artists, tapestries and bronzes, and a vault to hold jewelry were included in the luxurious Washington home of the Holladays.

But even "kings" face rough spots along the road of life, and Holladay was no exception. Though he earned as much as a million dollars each year for his mail contract, his profits were small. And the popularity of stagecoaches decreased after completion of the transcontinental railroad.

Holladay operated the central route and side routes to interior towns along the Overland Trail. In March of 1866, he purchased the Butterfield lines, which included most of the southern route contracts.

The Butterfield Company used one hundred Concord spring wagons and coaches.

Holladay bought only the best, and when he sold his line to Wells Fargo in 1866, he controlled three thousand miles of daily stage lines and five thousand miles of mail contracts. Wells Fargo then monopolized the transportation and mail businesses on the central route until locomotives replaced stagecoaches as the popular mode of travel.

Holladay's wife, Ann, died at Ophir Place and was first buried in the family chapel nearby. Later when the mansion was sold at public auction due to the loss of a western railroad, her body was moved to Rye, New York.

Holladay himself turned to seek his dreams in the West. After retiring from the stagecoach business, he became involved with Oregon businesses, such as a large sawmill at Portland and a hotel located near the city. Another disappointment came in the form of a failed California railroad promotion, caused in part by the Panic of 1873.

Ben Holladay married a second time, after he had moved west. He and his wife, Esther, produced two children, Ben C. and Linda.

Holladay's journey through life came to an end on July 7, 1887. Esther died April 5, 1889.

His stagecoaches carried people across the Overland Trail, introducing them to such places as Fort Halleck and Sulphur Springs, places teeming with the adventure of the frontier that would eventually become a part of Carbon County, Wyoming, and lead other people to their destinations.

E.W. Bennett

EMIGRANTS FOLLOWED THE trails blazed by Jim Baker and other scouts and explorers of the time. They traveled through the frontier, westward toward their destinies, experiencing their own adventures along the way.

Many of the emigrants traveled along the Overland Trail, their treasured belongings and precious provisions packed into wagons. They would have to cross rivers, among them the North Platte, and those crossings often proved hazardous.

Signatures in sandstone rocks at Emigrant's Crossing, located today on private property, can still be seen. Several graves remain in the area, testimony to the hazards of trail travel of more than a century ago.

Bennett's Ferry carried travelers safely across the North Platte, in an area north of the present day town of Saratoga. The North Platte River crossing is marked today by a stone monument erected along Wyoming Highway 130 south of Walcott, about nine miles from the actual crossing. The marker was placed by the Wyoming Landmarks Commission, with cooperation from several local organizations.

E. W. "Ed" Bennett was involved in several business ventures after he settled at the North Platte River Crossing in July 1864. He had previously served with the Twenty-sixth Regiment of the Iowa Volunteer Infantry during the Civil War.

Bennett worked as a "bullwhacker" driving a team of bulls along the Overland Trail west to Salt Lake City, so he was familiar with the trail when he arrived in the Carbon County area that autumn.

Bennett, along with two partners, also took a grading contract with the Union Pacific, preparing the road for the railroad track layers, according to Gay Day Alcorn in her book, *Tough Country*.

31

Bennett's first ferry effort was not successful, but his second try at the ferrying business became known as Bennett's Ferry.

His first ferrying venture, a partnership with a man named Tom Redrup (sometimes spelled Redrip), who had worked with Bennett on the railroad contract, included a general store. High spring run-off in 1867 washed out the ferry. The partnership ended too.

Bennett then moved two-and-a-half miles upriver, naming the ferry "Bennett's Ferry." Frank Earnest, Louis Reidsell, and "Boney" Earnest all helped run this ferry. Built with logs cut from trees on the banks of the river, it transported emigrants going west and east across the country.

Business boomed. Charging $5 per wagon, the ferry operators earned as much as $1,000 a day. As many as one hundred wagons waited on each side of the river to cross, and the ferry operators took the wagons across by twos.

Alcorn stated that William Henry Jackson, a well-known frontier photographer, took one of the first rides on the ferry in July 1867, while he was taking livestock east. Emigrants kept the ferry busy, as did the nearly seven thousand teamsters who regularly traveled along the trail. Often the ferry ran night and day.

A competing ferry began operating in North Platte City, near the site of Fort Fred Steele, a new military post which was soon to be constructed. This ferry only ran during daylight hours.

A letter from H.C. Overaker to Laramie's *Frontier Index* on June 12, 1868, presented a picture of North Platte City which differed from the bustling activities at Bennett's Ferry.

Overaker stated, "Business very dull; I have only seen two dollars change hands since I have been here; nothing doing in the grocery business." He went on to say that goods were sold for cheaper prices at the crossing than they were in Cheyenne.

At the time of Overaker's letter, the river was rising "at the rate of two feet per hour, and the town is liable to be under water at any moment, as it is located on the banks of the river."

The town of North Platte City did succumb to flooding; its demise was reported in a subsequent issue of the *Frontier Index*.

Engineers were just beginning to lay out the town of Brownsville about two-and-one-half miles from the crossing, and Overaker's letter stated, "Indians have commenced depredations again. Twenty were seen yesterday near here in full colors, and ready for a fight. That is all the excitement there has been here for the last ten days."

Residents of North Platte City relocated to Brownsville after the flooding. At Bennett's Ferry, though, people were still traveling the Overland Trail and using the ferry to cross the North Platte. The profitable business held little glamour against the possibility of a hefty gold strike, however.

In 1868, Bennett and his partners caught the wanderlust. Bennett sold out his goods and left his ranch and the ferry to search for gold. The rush was on in South Pass, Wyoming Territory. He built a twenty thousand dollar hotel there, which he ran with partners until the fall of 1869.

The April 2, 1903, issue of the *Saratoga Sun* reported, "Would be miners were starving and the Indian trouble was getting worse. [Bennett and his partners] just pulled out and left the hotel and went back to their spot on the North Platte and started to run the ferry and the old ranch again. They again made plenty of money."

Bennett soon contracted to haul freight to the Ute Indian Agency on the White River at Meeker, Colorado. In 1879, he earned the mail contract between Rawlins and the agency. The contract was abandoned when the Ute War broke out.

He married Phoebe Jane Noble of Iowa on April 8, 1872. Bennett had known her family for fifteen years. According to Alcorn, "This brilliant young woman had been well-educated and cultivated and was ready to take her place in a gracious Eastern society. Instead, she came with her new husband to make their home on the bank of a river in the wilderness."

The couple's daughters, Edna and Ellen, like many frontier children, were first educated by their mother when they were very young. They later attended school at Fort Steele, traveling to their classes on the backs of their pet calves.

In 1873, when Taylor Pennock moved to the area around Bennett's Ferry, he shot and sold antelope to emigrants crossing the river. Nearly a hundred wagons still crossed daily.

Bennett's Ferry had a little more luck than the ill-fated North Platte City. It grew into a town with a post office in 1878. Frank

Earnest was appointed as postmaster. An 1879 Department of the Interior map showed Bennett's Ferry listed as a town in the Territory of Wyoming.

Not everyone thought a ferry was so necessary. Alcorn related a tragic experience recalled by Bennett's daughter, Edna. An emigrant wanted to cross the river with his wagon, family, and animals but refused to pay the five dollar fee. He considered it too expensive. He took his family into the river with the wagon, which capsized in the high waters, killing everyone before the ferryman and the crew could help them.

Bennett recounted some of the "yarns" that he learned from the travelers in a 1932 issue of the *Saratoga Sun*. One of the yarns was first told in the July 14, 1891, issue of the *Sun*, and concerned a gold prospector.

"In 1868, when Ed Bennett ran the stage ferry on the old Emigrant Trail on the North Platte River, he had a strange visitor in an old treasure-hunter who raised great expectations by the promise of showing him the rich gold diggings on the east slope of the Sierra Madre range, and not far away."

During the first snowstorm of that season, in late September or early October, an elderly man knocked on Bennett's door at the stage station. Bennett was enjoying a smoke after supper.

The man was ill with mountain fever, so Bennett invited him inside and made him comfortable, then tended to his livestock— two packhorses and a saddle horse, all in good condition.

Bennett returned inside, where he made supper for the ill man, who could only drink coffee.

"The only explanation the patient gave was that he had been at work in the mountains but was forced to leave on account of his feebleness and for lack of provisions, his supplies being entirely exhausted," the *Sun* reported. The next day, the man's condition had improved but he didn't talk much about himself. He remained at the stage station for several days, then decided to set out for Laramie.

Bennett decided that the man was an unlucky prospector and told him his account was square. The man expressed much appreciation for the kindness shown him and said that Bennett had saved his life.

He paid for his lodgings and care with a bag of gold, saying it came from the direction of the Sierra Madre Mountains and that it wasn't a bad haul for only five days of work. He was very secretive and stingy with information, and he never revealed his name.

He did not tell Bennett the exact location of his diggings, but left for Laramie, saying that he'd ship lumber to Fort Steele in the spring to build a flume and sluice boxes. He promised to take Bennett to the claim when he returned.

He was never seen nor heard from again.

"The advent of the aged treasure-trove character in this section was prior to the time that Bennett heard anything about the lost Bradfield diggings," the *Sun* reported, referring to a better known "lost" gold claim. "Neither Bradfield, nor any of the old prospectors who accompanied him on his expeditions,…professed to know anything about the mysterious gold-washer [whom Bennett encountered]."

Bennett also brushed elbows with dignitaries. In 1878, "Wyoming Webb" C. Hayes, the son of President Rutherford B. Hayes, participated in General Crook's hunt in the Wyoming Territory. Young Hayes bagged an elk, a blacktail deer, six antelope, and ducks. He stopped at E. W. Bennett's ranch before traveling on to Fort Steele, according to Alcorn's history.

Bennett actively participated in Territorial politics. He served on the board of Carbon County Commissioners in 1870. He was elected to the Council of the Wyoming Legislature in 1882, represented Carbon County in the House, and in 1884 was re-elected to the Council.

He enjoyed horse racing, which Alcorn stated was "a prime feature for local people, just as it was at Saratoga Springs, New York." Bennett's horse "Grey Eagle" raced in the 1880s against other county horses. Bets ran as high as a thousand dollars, with Bennett wagering "several million dollars more or less."

By 1882 the sport attracted much attention and "throughout the whole decade thousands of dollars changed hands," Alcorn reported. "It seemed the only thing Platte Valley people enjoyed more than dancing was a good horse race."

Bennett, one of the first permanent settlers of the area in 1866, made his mark on Carbon County by ferrying emigrants across the

North Platte River, by serving in political offices, and through his generous spirit.

"Ed Bennett was liked by all who knew him," the April 2, 1903, edition of the *Saratoga Sun* stated. "He was held in high esteem and his friends numbered in the thousands. The saying went, 'When Bennett had money, everyone had money.' He was very generous."

Richard I. Dodge

RICHARD IRVING DODGE established Fort Fred Steele on the southern edge of the Red Desert and along the northern edges of the Platte River Valley in June 1868. Encompassing an area thirty-six miles square, the fort's mission was to protect the swiftly advancing transcontinental railroad.

Dodge became the new fort's first commanding officer.

Some confusion exists about the exact date of the fort's establishment. Dodge indicated on post returns from the fort that the date was June 15, 1868; however, most sources list it as June 30, 1868. The area was surveyed in early June.

Colonel Dodge served in the Thirtieth Infantry when Fort Steele held its largest garrison. The fort earned its name from Major-General Frederick Steele, a Mexican War and Civil War veteran who died the year the fort was established. The fort's first commanding officer had his hands full battling the Indians in the area.

In *Tough Country*, Gay Day Alcorn wrote, "For centuries the Native Americans' lives remained the same in the remote territory, and change was not welcomed. The post, therefore, was brought to life in a battle of arrows, bullets, and blood...."

Construction on the fort, located "in the midst of the most warlike and uncivilized Indians of the plains, according to Dodge," progressed slowly as the troops fought the Indians.

The construction created economic progress in the area. Dodge sent Company G to the Warm Springs area, which later became known as Saratoga, to guard woodcutters while they made railroad ties and lumber for the new fort. The loggers worked on Elk Mountain and in the Grand Encampment Valley.

As the railroad raced westward, towns sprang up along the tracks, some of them notorious, and some of them located on the military reservation controlled by Fort Fred Steele. The end-of-the-tracks towns, sometimes known as "hell on wheels," earned reputations for murders and other dastardly deeds. Shootings occurred daily in such towns.

The diverse group of people who settled in the usually short-lived towns often lived in tents. Folks from all walks of life lived there, including railroad workers, gold diggers, soiled doves, travelers, emigrants, Indians, mountain men, and gamblers.

Laramie City, an end-of-the-tracks town, survived to become Laramie even after many people moved on ahead to Brownsville. Brownsville, located on the Fort Steele military reservation, caused such a stir that Commanding Officer Dodge ordered its residents to move to a new town site across the river. The new town, Benton, was located three miles down the railroad line.

Anyone who disobeyed Dodge's orders was placed in the new guardhouse at Fort Steele. Benton lasted only a few months that summer of 1868, as Rawlins Springs was soon chosen as the railroad's division point. Though Benton's life was brief, its notorious reputation earned it a secure place in Wyoming's history. Nothing but some nails, broken glass, and the alkali dust it was built on remains of Benton, now located on private property.

Dodge did not remain at Fort Steele very long, either, staying only to see its sound establishment. The Official Army Register of 1895 showed a transfer in March of 1869. The fort remained in use until 1886.

Today, remains of the fort include the old stone corral, the stone chimneys of the barracks, the bridge tender's house, the ordnance, the fort sutler's home, and the cemetery. Fort Steele, a Wyoming historic site and on the National Register of Historic Places, is located about one and one-half miles off Interstate 80. It is open to the public during the summer months.

🐚🐚🐚

Richard Irving Dodge graduated from the United States Military Academy twenty years before the construction of Fort Steele began. Born in western North Carolina in 1827, Dodge grew to have not only a military career but also to become an author. He penned four books during his lifetime—*Our Wild Indians, Plains of the Great West, The Black Hills*, and *A Living Issue*.

Prior to the Civil War, Dodge served in western posts. During the war, he served in administrative positions, earning a promotion to Lieutenant Colonel in 1873.

He served as the military escort commander protecting geologists during the 1875 Black Hills expedition, an experience prompting him to keep a journal on which to base his official report. Though scientific findings and conclusions were published in his report of the expedition, Dodge's journal remained unpublished for nearly a century.

His book, *The Black Hills*, published in 1876, was considered promotional. In 1975, Lesta V. Turchen and James D. McLaird reprinted his report, closely tied to its original form, in a book entitled, *The Black Hills Expedition of 1875*. McLaird, a history professor at Dakota Wesleyan University in Mitchell, South Dakota, noted two recent books edited by Wayne Kime that contain Dodge's recently discovered personal diaries. These newer books reveal more of the colonel's personality through his descriptions of the people as well as the landscapes. The books are *The Black Hills Journals of Colonel Richard Irving Dodge* and *The Powder River Expedition Journals of Colonel Richard Irving Dodge*, both recently released from the University of Oklahoma Press.

Dodge outlined what was then a controversial plan in *Our Wild Indians*. His plan advocated the breakup of treaty systems and tribal relations in favor of absorbing Indians as individuals into "the great family of American citizens."

He wrote, "My earliest recollections are tinged with stories of Indian atrocities, for the Cherokees yet occupied 'the land of their Fathers,' and were only a short distance from us." Though the Indians "had committed no outrages," the white people lived in "constant dread" and demanded their removal from the state.

Dodge felt that Indians should become American citizens. He wrote, "There is no future for the Indian as Indian; but I can see for him long vistas of honor and usefulness when he shall have become a citizen of the United States. If we had said to the Irish or to the

Germans, 'You may live among us but you shall never be citizens,' would we have been as great a nation to-day?"

Dodge was twice brevetted for meritorious service, retiring from military service in 1891. He died June 16, 1895, in Sacketts Harbor, New York.

Philippe Regis de Trobriand

As AN ARTIST, HE USED contrast in colors and shadings to create his impression of the area around Fort Fred Steele. In his personal life, Philippe Regis de Trobriand experienced vivid contrasts, ranging from the elegance of Parisian society in the late 1800s to the spartan accommodations of the frontier of the American West.

Artist, author, composer, father, military man—each of these terms describes de Trobriand, who commanded Fort Steele from 1871 until 1874. The Frenchman was brevetted to Major General during his United States military career. The only other Frenchman to achieve such high rank in this country was Lafayette.

De Trobriand's artistic works include two oil paintings of Fort Steele, currently kept in a collection at the Wyoming State Museum. His written works, *Quatre ans a l'Armee du Potomac* (translated and published in 1889 as *Four Years with the Army of the Potomac)* and *Military Life in Dakota*, unfortunately do not contain information on his experiences in Wyoming. He also penned an earlier novel, *Les Gentilshommes de l'Quest*, written during his term as the Minister of the Interior in Paris. His oldest daughter, Marie Caroline de Trobriand Post, wrote his life history, entitled *The Life and Memoire of Comte Regis de Trobriand*, which was published in 1910.

Caroline's book sheds some light on the Major General's personality through the series of letters she received from her father. She wrote, "While the rest of the biography is written to depict General de Trobriand's many sided character as a man of the world, a man of talents, and a man of intellect, his letters to his daughter give a glimpse of his power of devotion and love as a man of heart."

Caroline, who the General affectionately called "Lina," kept nearly every letter he sent to her until his death. "These experiences of a soldier writing to his daughter are uncommon war documents; as the letters of my father to me, they are part of his heart history," she wrote.

🐝🐝🐝

Philippe Regis Denis de Keredern de Trobriand was born June 4, 1816, near Tours, France. His father, one of Napoleon's generals, was given command of the city of Toulouse, and young Regis, at six years old the eldest son, joined his father.

His mother died in 1832. Raised as a page in the royal household, Regis received an excellent education. He surprised his military family by choosing to study law, and he graduated from Poitiers and earned admission to the bar in 1837.

His father died in 1840. Regis became a Baron. He did not practice law but earned a position with the French Ministry of the Interior. While there, he wrote his first book, *Les Gentilshommes de l'Quest,* a novel.

In 1841, the young Baron sailed to New York with his friend, the Comte de McCarty, who was originally from New Orleans. He traveled throughout the United States and Canada for a year. While in America, he met Mary Mason Jones, daughter of the President of Chemical Bank of New York.

That meeting proved to be fortuitous. The couple were married in France in 1843 and traveled through Europe the next year. They made their permanent home in New York in 1848, but their marriage would not succeed. Years later, they became estranged. Mary traveled with their other daughter, Beatrice, to live in France.

Caroline wrote that during the years from 1847 to 1861 de Trobriand devoted much time to music, writing, and painting. Composers both abroad and in America set his words to music.

In 1854, after spending three years in France, de Trobriand returned to America where he became sub-editor of *Le Courrier des Etats Unis.* He wrote a regular weekly column chronicling social, literary, and artistic events from 1854 until 1861.

De Trobriand was in New York in April 1861, when the Civil War began. On July 21, the day before the battle of Bull Run, he was unanimously elected Colonel of the Gardes Lafayette (Fifty-fifth Regiment). De Trobriand became an American citizen and an officer of the U. S. Volunteer Army. He was notified of his election as Colonel of the Gardes Lafayette (Fifty-fifth Regiment) while he completed a painting of Venice's grand canal.

During his war service, de Trobriand fought in the Battle of Chancellorsville, the Battle of Gettysburg, and the fight of Manassas Gap in 1863. He was appointed the Brigadier General of Volunteers in January 1864 and assigned to the command of the First Brigade Third Division and Corps of the Army of the Potomac in July. In April 1865, he participated in skirmishes at Farmville and Highbridge, with an afternoon engagement of his command on the main road to Appomattox Courthouse. In January 1866, he mustered out of the volunteer service and returned to Paris.

The notes he kept during the war eventually became his book, *Quatre ans a l'Armee du Potomac.* The account was later translated by George K. Dauchy and published in 1889 as *Four Years with the Army of the Potomac.*

De Trobriand left Paris in 1867 and returned once again to the United States. Napoleon III reigned over the Empire of France. De Trobriand traveled to Fort Stevenson, Dakota, where he rejoined his regiment. The trip included twenty days' travel up the Missouri River. In the wilderness, he used tents and temporary log cabins for shelter. This frontier life contrasted vividly with Parisian life.

De Trobriand found ways to adapt to his new environment. He seemed equally at ease with frontiersmen, Indians, and dignitaries, a skill which served him well throughout his life. Though three tribes of friendly Indians lived near the fort—the Arikara, Gros Ventres, and Mandan—the Sioux resisted the military presence. Caroline stated that Sitting Bull, the Sioux Chief, "gave General de Trobriand much trouble."

The General spent two years in the northern Dakota Territory, struggling through frigid cold and deep snows. He spent many hours painting, and he studied Sioux dialect. The skill helped him to communicate directly with the Indians rather than rely on an interpreter. He sketched portraits of Sitting Bull and other Indian chiefs.

Included in de Trobriand's journal are other anecdotes about hunting expeditions, a bad January snowstorm, and a prairie fire that threatened the fort. The journal eventually became his book, *Military Life in Dakota*. When the army was reduced in 1869 to twenty-five regiments, de Trobriand stopped keeping his journal. He was appointed Colonel of the Thirteenth Infantry.

Caroline wrote, "The General's time of service in Wyoming was void of stirring events such as marked the years spent in Dakota, Montana, and Utah, but in Wyoming there were great hunting expeditions, and during the long winter evenings he added German to his list of accomplishments."

He took command of Fort Steele in 1871, a position he held until 1874. Caroline wrote, "The Districts under the General's command in those years were the 'Wild West,' where the Vigilantes did the work of judge and jury, and where the line of the railroad was as plainly indicated by mounds of new-made graves, as by the track of steel rail laid by their occupants before they 'died in their boots.' The General had many interesting experiences with these desperadoes, but never any trouble, for they knew he was not to be trifled with."

When Caroline was tragically widowed in 1872, de Trobriand traveled to New York City to be with her. He stayed with her for six weeks.

During his absence from Fort Steele, a series of fires destroyed several buildings. A fire burned the guardhouse, a defective flue started a fire which destroyed the bakery, and General de Trobriand's stables burned in late July. Three of his prize horses were killed in the fire. Another fire in mid-August destroyed the carpenter shop. The fires were considered the work of an arsonist. The General returned in mid-September, and no further fires plagued the post until nearly ten years later.

In 1873, France had become a republic, and Thiers was president. General de Trobriand was appointed to present to Thiers an address signed by thousands of French citizens of New York who were grateful for the liberation of France. The General requested and received permission from his military superiors in the United States to take a year's leave of absence to travel to France to present the document and visit family. General Sherman, who was then serving as the Secretary of War, wrote that "there can be no possible objection to your doing this."

Caroline stated that the winter of 1873–74 was "one of rare enjoyment" to her father. He was able to renew old friendships and visit with relatives and mingle with the distinguished men of Parisian society and artists and writers. "Truly it was a contrast with life in the Western wilds of America," she wrote.

De Trobriand also donated Indian memorabilia to the museum in his hometown of Tours, France. He gave two complete outfits for an Indian man and woman along with war items and domestic utensils. Caroline wrote that on the General's next visit to the museum, he saw models dressed in the clothes. The garments lost something in the translation, though a spark of humor was added. The man's tribal regalia was worn by a model sporting a flowing mustache.

In the spring of 1874, Caroline joined her father in Paris. When de Trobriand's childless cousin, the Comte Adolphe de Trobriand, died, the General succeeded to the title of Count and became the official head of his family.

The General returned to the United States in October. His regiment was ordered to New Orleans, where conflict over reconstruction politics brewed. Democrats and Republicans were practically at war over election results, and President Grant dispatched federal troops to restore order at the request of Louisiana officials. It fell to General de Trobriand to arrest the members of one of two Louisiana Legislatures meeting at the time.

De Trobriand retired in 1879, spending the summers of his retirement years in Paris and Bayport, Long Island, and wintering in New Orleans, Louisiana.

General de Trobriand met with General Sherman in September, 1890, a few months before Sherman's death. At Grey Towers, the home of Mr. and Mrs. James Pinchot in Milford, Pennsylvania, the two men planted trees and enjoyed what would be their final visit. De Trobriand died in 1897 in New Orleans.

✻❀✻

"....One case of scarlet fever occurred in the Post this week, in the family of Private Sweeney, which resulted in death. A sharp look out has been kept in order to prevent the spreading of the disease."

"The boys are waiting very patiently for the Paymaster, and anticipate a 'boss' time with their two months earnings. Glorious drunks will be plentiful and sore heads divers, the guard house well represented and 'blinds' numerous."

"Cold. Tramps scarce. The new store looks well. The new post office must be seen to be appreciated.... We undoubtedly have the handsomest store and by far the best post office in Carbon county, you should see it, elegance reigns supreme, comfort, and utility combined; and the Judge with his hands in his pockets, proud as a peacock, takes the praise well earned very quietly. But he cannot stand the phrenologist yet a while....Me at the pump house enjoys music and is ready at any or all times to do his share in promoting the same. Never mind, Me, you shall have another concert sometime in good old U. P. style."

From "Fort Steele Items,"
Carbon County Journal, March 13 and September 18, 1880

Thomas Tipton Thornburgh

AT THIRTY-TWO, HE BECAME ONE of the youngest military officers to earn the rank of major. His transfer from the paymaster corps to the position of commanding officer at Fort Fred Steele in 1878 foreboded impending disaster.

By the late 1870s, the fort's purpose—protecting the transcontinental railroad—had been served. Railroad crews had finished work years before, and locomotives chugged steadily across the Wyoming Territory. Indian hostilities, for the most part, seemed to have been resolved in the area.

Marshall Sprague wrote in *Massacre: The Tragedy at White River,* "General Crook had told Thornburgh frankly that the post served no military purpose whatsoever." Crook thought the fort would be abandoned and decided to soon transfer Thornburgh from Fort Steele to a post which offered more "adventure."

Unfortunately, before Thornburgh could be transferred, his assignment at Fort Steele would provide at least one adventure, one which would become the major's final experience.

❦

Nathan Meeker, the agent at the White River Indian Agency across the border in Colorado, was finding it difficult to get along with the Ute Indians there.

Meeker began his assignment at the agency in 1878, but his ideas were unpopular with the Indians. He hoped to teach them agriculture and advocated teaching their children the English language and American customs. He discouraged their recreational horse racing and summer hunting trips. The United States government supported his ideas but did not send any troops to enforce them.

Major T.T. Thornburgh. (Courtesy Wyoming Division of Cultural Resources)

By the time Major Thornburgh received orders in 1879 to take troops to the White River Agency to enforce peace, tempers were flaring to the boiling point. The major hoped to resolve the difficulties without violence. Ironically, he became the first man to lose his life in the resulting battle. He died September 29, 1879, the victim of a bullet shot from an Indian's rifle.

The *Cheyenne Daily Leader* of October 3, 1879, reported, "[Major] Thornburgh had many warm friends in this city who deeply regret his death. He was a gallant officer and a genial warmhearted gentleman."

The boy who would grow into that "gallant" officer was born the day after Christmas 1843, in New Market, Tennessee. His parents were Montgomery and Olivia Anne Thornburgh.

Montgomery Thornburgh served as a Democrat in the Tennessee Legislature, and he fought hard to keep his state as part of the Union. An opponent of slavery, he died of starvation at Andersonville Prison at the age of forty-five, according to Sprague.

His young son, nicknamed "Tip," soon displayed his own fighting spirit. In September 1861, he left home to join the Sixth Regiment of Tennessee Volunteers, wanting to fight with the Union forces. This, of course, was against the wishes of his mother. Tip enlisted as a private at age eighteen.

The young man was a crack shot, having learned from his father, and he soon earned a promotion to sergeant major. He moved up the ranks, becoming a lieutenant and then an adjutant. He fought in the Battle of Millspring and was present during General Morgan's retreat from Cumberland Gap to the Ohio River.

He garnered a more formal military education as well. Thornburgh graduated from West Point in 1867, taking an assignment with the Second Artillery at the Presidio in San Francisco, California, until early the next year.

He attended artillery school from April 13, 1868, to May of the next year at Fortress Monroe, Virginia. The young officer received the privilege of serving as Aide to the Grand Marshal in the second inaugural parade of President U.S. Grant. He also served for a short time in Sitka, Alaska. In 1870, he was promoted to second lieutenant.

During his assignment to Fortress Monroe, he had met Lida Clarke, the sister of one of his friends. They were married on his twenty-seventh birthday in 1870 at Fort Omaha, where Lida's father served as an Army paymaster. After their brief honeymoon in San Francisco, Thornburgh worked at Alcatraz, California, until late 1871. He also served briefly as a professor of military science in San Diego. From 1871 to 1873, he taught military tactics at East Tennessee University in Knoxville.

He steadily advanced throughout his military career. After serving as a professor at Knoxville, he served in the Fort Foote, Maryland, garrison until 1875. His rank then became first lieutenant of artillery.

Thornburgh still wasn't satisfied. He aspired to achieve even higher ranks.

The lowest rank in the paymaster corps was that of Major. He applied for a vacancy in the corps and was soon assigned the position of paymaster in San Antonio, Texas.

He was stationed in Fort Omaha for a little more than a year but the paymaster corps didn't offer the kind of excitement that a young, well-trained military man desired.

According to Sprague, Thornburgh participated in a shooting match in Omaha with the "renowned Dr. Frank Carver." The match, which was really just for fun, lasted only about an hour. Carver won, but General George Crook was in the audience and admired Thornburgh's skill. Soon, Thornburgh was traveling west with the general to participate in hunts. The hunting expeditions took them as far as Fort Bridger and probably led to Thornburgh's interest in the area that is now Carbon County.

🌺

When Thornburgh earned the commander's position at Fort Fred Steele, he allowed the soldiers there to enjoy themselves some. There were dances and hunting trips, and everyone was allowed to watch the sun's total eclipse on September 10, 1878.

No one then could have realized that the shadowed sun would signal darker days in the year ahead.

Some of Thornburgh's dark days resulted from an expedition for General Crook he led into Nebraska that fall which failed. The purpose of the mission was to stop two bands of Cheyenne Indians from escaping to the north. Foggy weather and a mechanical problem with the troop train became insurmountable obstacles.

Thornburgh was not criticized for the failed mission, according to Sprague, but he felt he had disappointed the general. Thornburgh was determined not to let the general down again, and he "made meticulous plans for a successful White River expedition" should he be called to the agency to assist Nathan Meeker.

Thornburgh had been receiving messages from Meeker, requesting help with his Indian difficulties and asking for assistance from the troops at Fort Steele. Though Thornburgh forwarded these messages to his superiors, he didn't receive orders to send troops to the White River Agency until the problems had escalated.

🌺

Thornburgh managed to eke out some enjoyment during his time in Wyoming Territory. He loved to hunt and enjoyed the outdoors. Since no orders to action seemed forthcoming, he joined thirteen men in a hunting expedition to the Sierra Madre Mountains near present-day Encampment. Other members of the prestigious group included Webb Hayes, the son of President Rutherford B. Hayes; General Crook; and Dr. John Draper, a famous urologist. They camped in a scenic area near Battle Lake. Thornburgh was said to have great luck, catching fifty-two fish in thirty minutes.

The area had a reputation with important men from the east coast. The previous year, 1878, while camped near this same Battle Lake area on a similar hunting expedition, Thomas Edison conceived the idea for the incandescent filament light bulb. Today, a monument at Battle Pass of Highway 70 commemorates the event.

On a later hunting trip to the same area, Thornburgh received the orders he'd awaited—to take troops to the White River Agency to assist Nathan Meeker. Hunting with him were his older brother, Jake, who had become a congressman, two Tennessee bankers, and Taylor Pennock, who served as their guide.

Thornburgh wanted Pennock to return to the fort with him to guide the troops to the White River Agency, since Pennock was highly skilled and well-versed in the area. However, a bit of sibling rivalry reared its head, and Jake insisted that the hunters continue on, keeping Pennock as their guide.

So, another man who would figure prominently in the history of the region became Thornburgh's guide—Joe Rankin. Captain J. Scott Payne served as Thornburgh's second-in-command for the mission.

The troops left Fort Steele on September 22, 1879. The convoy consisted of three calvary troops, one infantry company, and a thirty-three wagon supply train.

Much has been written about the ensuing battle between the Utes and the Fort Steele troops, and perspectives have changed with time.

According to an article written by Major M. C. Harrington, retired, in the December 1929 issue of the *Cactus,* from two to three thousand Ute Indians, armed with rifles and ammunition furnished by the government, met Thornburgh's troops. Other sources number the Indians at four hundred or fewer.

Sub-Chief Indian Jack pretended to be hunting when he met the troops about sixty miles from the White River Agency, but offered to take Thornburgh to the agency to talk to the other Indian leaders. Thornburgh refused, not realizing that Indian Jack had hidden nearly three hundred of his warriors in the area.

Still hoping for a peaceful resolution, Thornburgh advanced with a white flag, calling for a retreat when his own officers warned him of the danger surrounding them. Harrington reported that Thornburgh and thirteen soldiers were killed when the Indians began shooting.

Sprague offered a slightly different picture, stating that Rankin and Lieutenant Cherry rode ahead of the troops, finding fresh campfire ashes after crossing Milk Creek. Thornburgh decided the troops should travel to Beaver Springs, five miles inside the borders of the reservation, near Yellowjacket Pass. Beaver Springs held the nearest water supply.

The troops still had several miles of travel ahead when Rankin and Cherry warned of danger. Rankin reported to Thornburgh that Indians had topped the ridge and planned an ambush.

Historian Sprague agrees with Harrington's view that Thornburgh sought peaceful resolution to the problems. He wrote that Thornburgh rode out and waved to the Indians, who waved back. Cherry waved, too, but his wave was mistaken as a battle sign and all hell broke loose.

According to Sprague, Thornburgh went through the woods to check the location of the supply train as the Indians came down the ridge. He lost his life when a bullet struck him above the ear. Dr. Mark Miller's research indicates that Thornburgh's wound was to the chest. All agree that Thornburgh died of wounds resulting from the battle. He was only 35 years old.

Nathan Meeker was killed before the battle was over.

The Utes were eventually sent to a reservation in Utah. Chief Ouray later returned to their families the women and children who had been taken by the Indians. Disagreement about the causes and details of the battle continued for years. Discussion of the battle at the White River Agency still fosters feelings of sadness and regret at the loss of life which occurred there.

Thomas Tipton Thornburgh's funeral was held October 22, 1879, in Omaha, with nearly thirty thousand attending the solemn service. He was buried at the Prospect Hill Cemetery, though his casket was not the only one lowered into the ground on that day. The body of his son, George Washington Thornburgh, who had died that same year at age three, was exhumed from the cemetery at Fort Fred Steele and reburied at Omaha. The younger Thornburgh's casket was buried on top of his father's.

Thornburgh was posthumously cited for gallantry, and a street in Laramie carried his name for many years. The street's name was changed in the late 1920s to honor Edward Ivinson, a man who had helped with the development of Laramie.

The name change stirred controversy, and the oldest citizen living on Thornburgh Street at that time, M.C. Brown, an Albany County pioneer, voiced his opposition through an article published in the *Wyoming Eagle*. Brown called Thornburgh "a brave and gallant soldier." Brown had lived on Thornburgh Street for more than fifty years.

Lida Thornburgh never remarried. She lived in Washington, D.C., and also in Oakland, Maryland, prior to her death in 1930 in Manhattan, Kansas.

"Rankin did not stop. From this point he went by way of the Mora-pos trail, riding as fast as possible for safety over the rough trail in the night. He reached the Hulett and Torrence cattle camp on Bear River in the early morning, where he procured a fresh mount.... Crossing Bear River at this point, he went by way of Fortification Creek, reaching the road near the Thornburgh reserve camp, where he advised Lieutenant Price of the disaster.

...[Rankin] arrived in Rawlins at two A.M., October first. This distance is approximately one hundred and fifty miles. The time, including stops, was twenty-seven and one-half hours."

From *Reminiscences of Frontier Days,*
by M. Wilson Rankin,
on file at the Wyoming State Museum

Joe Rankin

IN THE HISTORY OF OUR COUNTRY, urgency mixed with a man and a horse often equals thrilling and dangerous feats. Sometimes it spells disaster. In Joe Rankin's case, the ingredients combined to create an oft-told story which showcases a hero.

Joe Rankin's name is mentioned often in the history of not one, but two, Wyoming counties. Rankin's memorable achievements are connected with Carbon County and Johnson County.

In Carbon County's history, Rankin is perhaps best remembered for a heroic ride from the White River Agency in Colorado to Rawlins to obtain rescue forces for Major Thornburgh's troops.

Legends grow and change with time, and so it is with the remarkable horseback ride made by Joe Rankin. Sprague, in his book, *Massacre: The Tragedy at White River*, aptly described Rankin as "Carbon County's Paul Revere."

In a little more than twenty-seven hours, Rankin raced from the White River Agency to Rawlins, about 150 miles, to send the devastating message of the Ute Indians' attack against the troops commanded by Major Thomas T. Thornburgh of Fort Steele. The sad message also contained news of the young Major's death in the battle.

Accounts of the ride differ a little, however. Some state that Rankin walked the whole way. Some accounts record the duration of the event as twenty-eight hours; some state that Rankin sensed the danger before Thornburgh arrived on the scene; and others report that Rankin went along with Thornburgh as a guide.

The latter is probably the case, as that information came from the War Department, according to W. O. Owen, an Albany County surveyor who was surveying areas in Carbon County in 1879.

Owen wrote a pamphlet entitled, *Jo Rankin's Great Ride,* to set the record straight and to give Rankin, whom he considered a "warm friend," recognition for the remarkable journey.

Owen stated that Rankin traveled alone, which contradicts other accounts. He apparently left the massacre site on a wounded horse. Rankin used four horses on the trip, walking only when one of those horses collapsed. He was then forced to walk ahead a few miles to secure another horse.

Owen reprinted a letter written to him in 1932 by R.M. Galbraith, an old-time Rawlins area resident and a mechanic for the Union Pacific. Galbraith said that he was in the Rawlins telegraph office at the time Rankin arrived, about midnight.

Sprague, in an article entitled, *Hero on Horseback,* published in the June 16, 1957, issue of the *Denver Post Empire Magazine,* stated that Rankin was on the scene at the massacre with Thornburgh's troops, helping them after their leader was killed. The second-in-command, Captain J. Scott Payne, requested volunteers for the ride to Rawlins, a mission considered highly risky because of the number of Ute Indians in the area.

Sprague said that four men volunteered—Rankin; John Gordon, a civilian freighter; and George Moquin and Ed Murphy, corporals. The men would be covered by pickets to the Rawlins road crossing. If Indians attacked, Rankin would ride alone cross-country while the others fought off the attackers.

Sprague reported that Rankin left at about 10:30 P.M. on Monday and arrived in Rawlins at 2 A.M. on Wednesday. Incongruous as it may seem, Sprague wrote that Rankin stopped in at Foote's Saloon for a drink before delivering the message to the telegraph office. Little Van, the bartender, bought drinks for the house, in recognition of the accomplishment.

Sprague clocked the journey at twenty-seven-and-a-half hours, as did M. Wilson Rankin in *Reminiscences of Frontier Days,* but Owens' account stated that Rankin had told him he didn't look at his watch but left a little before midnight and arrived about midnight the next day.

However the speedy ride was clocked, the somber message was sent and General Wesley Merritt from Fort Russell (near Cheyenne) arrived on the scene on October 5, 1879, with reinforcements.

🌺🌺🌺

But what about this heroic man who rocketed across the Wyoming Territory seeking rescue for Thornburgh's troops?

Joe Rankin was born in Armstrong County, Pennsylvania, in 1845. At sixteen, he enlisted to serve in the Civil War. Rankin was assigned to the Sixty-third Regiment of the Pennsylvania Volunteer Infantry and served through the war with distinction. He was discharged in 1864. After the war, he traveled to the oil region and became an oil roustabout near Pittsburgh.

Some of his other jobs included freighting in Sioux Indian country and gold mining near Deadwood, Central City, and Hahn's Peak.

Rankin came to Rawlins in 1872. He mined, becoming familiar with the Wyoming Territory and northern Colorado region. According to Sprague's article, he helped mine the native red pigment known as "Rawlins Red" which was used to paint the Brooklyn Bridge.

Owen said of Rankin, "He was an upright, outstanding citizen, modest and unassuming, a genial companion, perfectly unselfish, an admirable and lovable product of the great Western frontier, a prince among men."

Rankin also served as a member of the last Territorial Legislature from Carbon County. In 1890, when Wyoming achieved statehood, upon recommendation of U.S. Senators Joseph Carey and Francis E. Warren, Rankin was appointed U.S. Marshal for Wyoming by President Benjamin Harrison.

This appointment would test the heroic rider through the events surrounding a conflict that would gain national attention. During Rankin's term, the dispute known as the "Johnson County War" broke out. Historian T. A. Larson called the conflict "the most notorious event in the history of Wyoming."

Rankin, in his letter to the United States Attorney General in October 1892, stated that several events led to the war, including the hanging of James Averell and Ella "Cattle Kate" Watson.

The actual invasion took place in April 1892. Tempers on the range had flared because cattlemen with large herds had become very powerful. They considered the small ranchers and homesteaders to be usurpers of range which had traditionally been theirs to use; they put every possible roadblock in the way of homesteaders. Cattle thievery was rampant. Stray cattle belonging to homesteaders disappeared into the vast herds of the cattlemen. Cattlemen, in turn, suspected the homesteaders of rustling and hired stock detectives to guard their herds.

Lewis Gould wrote of the conflict in his article, *Francis Warren and the Johnson County War,* published in the magazine *Arizona and the West.* He stated, "Outraged by what they regarded as persistent rustling in northern Wyoming, prominent members of the Wyoming Stock Growers Association laid plans to send an expedition into Johnson County which would eliminate the major thieves." The stockmen left Cheyenne on April 5, bringing more than twenty Texas gunmen with them. Nathan Champion and Nick Ray, suspected of rustling, were killed.

The murders sent a warning to citizens of Johnson County, who "forced the invaders to seek refuge in the TA Ranch on Crazy Woman Creek," Gould stated. The two-day conflict drew the assistance of President Benjamin Harrison, who sent troops to rescue the cattlemen by taking them into custody.

In his letter, Rankin wrote, "There is a diversity of opinion as to the real purpose and grievance of the large cattlemen. They assert that the fight they are making is solely against cattle thieves, or rustlers. On the other hand, the people of Johnson County assert the belief, and this view is held by at least onehalf [*sic*] of the people of the state, that the fight is for the range; that every time a settler takes up one hundred and sixty acres of land, and especially when this is taken along one of the water courses, it just destroys to that extent the range for the large cattle owners and that it is to their interests to keep out actual settlers."

As marshal, Joe Rankin delayed the legal paper-serving which followed the conflict. F. E. Warren and Willis Van Devanter called for Joe Rankin's resignation on the grounds that the marshal had proven to be a coward. Rankin requested that the Justice Department investigate their accusations.

✻✻✻

Warren was a politician, having served as one of Wyoming's Territorial Governors and a legislator. He was elected as Wyoming's first governor after it achieved statehood in 1890, but resigned only a few months after his election to accept a position as United States Senator.

Gould wrote, "The political liabilities of the Johnson County War proved too much for Warren to overcome in 1892, but his Washington intrigues against Marshal Rankin were a brilliant early example of the method of a pork-barrel virtuoso and bureaucratic in-fighter unmatched in the history of the West."

The invasion created political repercussions. Wyoming Democrats accused the Republicans in the state's administration, especially Governor Amos W. Barber, of complicity in the stockmen's plan. Senators Warren and Joseph M. Carey faced accusations that they had participated in the scheme. Warren was up for re-election.

Rankin's job was to serve warrants against the homesteaders for conspiracy. Many believed the evidence was thin. This impending action, which would undoubtedly be met with resistance, put Rankin in position to request troops. He did not serve the warrants in June, declining because he did not have the help of the military.

President Harrison did not want to declare martial law and advised the use of civil process, suggesting that Rankin take enough deputies with him to serve the warrants.

Bureaucratic arguments continued for the next month or so, with Rankin feeling pressure to take a posse north. When the U.S Attorney General requested that Rankin either "act or give way to someone who will act," Rankin replied that he hadn't succeeded in assembling a group of deputies because of a lack of funds.

A message from President Harrison preceded Rankin's posse to Johnson County. The President ordered everyone who was resisting the laws and process of the United States to cease such actions and return to their homes.

The situation calmed. However on September 3, Warren and Carey requested that U.S. Attorney General Miller secure Rankin's resignation. Rankin, complaining of bad treatment by the press, requested a Justice Department investigation.

Rankin wrote to the Attorney General, stating, "The sentiment in this state is such today that the men, whom it would seem had represented to you that I have not performed my duty, and who, no doubt, are secretly asking for my removal, are afraid to come out openly and advocate it; but are themselves anxious and willing to have the matter held in abeyance until after the election." Rankin

Center forefront: Ben Northington. Front row, left to right: John Madden, George Wright, John Foote, and James Rankin. Back row, left to right: Mike Murphy, Joe Rankin, Tom Sun, and Boney Earnest. (Photo Courtesy Carbon County Museum. Identification: "100 Years of the Wild West," centennial supplement to the *Rawlins Daily Times,* 1968)

further stated that those men refused to put any charges against him in written form.

The Justice Department investigation cleared Rankin.

🐚🐚🐚

Joe Rankin's actions figured prominently in Wyoming's history, gaining him both compliments and criticism. On perhaps a quieter level, he established a stage line which ran from Rawlins to Saratoga and Gold Hill with his brothers. The Rankin Brothers line was first class, using six-horse Concord stages to make the daily fifty-mile trips.

He married Cornie E. Vail in Cheyenne on December 26, 1893. Rankin is also credited with helping found the Scottish Rite Masons in Wyoming. He died in 1919 and is buried in Ogden, Utah.

Isom Dart

EVERYONE EMBODIES SOME good qualities and some bad qualities. Most people usually display more of one than the other, and thus become recognized as either "good" or "bad." Isom Dart's life illustrates both his good and bad qualities. The cattle rustler tried to go straight several times, but never quite succeeded. John Rolfe Burroughs wrote in *Where the Old West Stayed Young* that Dart "loved thieving." He's remembered, however, as a kind man with an engaging personality. George Erhard, in a 1929 article in the *Rock Springs Rocket,* called Dart the "Gunga Din of Brown's Park."

Isom Dart came from a hill farm in the Arkansas Ozarks. He was born into slavery and was originally called Ned. He earned his freedom through the Emancipation Proclamation. At sixteen, he took his master's surname, Huddleston, and worked his way to the Rockies with a series of jobs, including rodeo clown, to support himself along the way.

Among his childhood friends was another man who would play a part in Carbon County history, W.G. "Billy" Tittsworth. Ned's master owned the farm adjoining Tittsworth's father's land. The two youngsters were the same age. Tittsworth, too, traveled west after the Civil War, where he hunted game to supply meat for stage stations along the Overland Trail and for the construction camps of the Union Pacific Railroad.

According to Burroughs, Tittsworth and Ned ran into each other at Carmichael Gap (Wilkins Station on the Union Pacific). Ned worked as a "pot walloper" for a Chinese cook there, and that resulted in a trip to jail, one in a series for him. The Chinese cook disappeared after a brawl over a crooked card game in which Ned had lost hundreds of dollars. Ned was locked in the Green River City jail, suspected of murder.

Jesse Ewing also spent that night in jail on suspicion of murder in another case. Ned and Ewing knew each other. Ewing had made a practice of luring men to his mine, taking their money and then leaving. Ned had been one of those men. Ewing and Ned had unfinished business; they fought that night, and Ewing beat Ned with his own boot.

But both men were released from jail the next day. It had been discovered that the man whom Ewing had been accused of killing had actually died of natural causes. And the Chinese cook had returned to the town, alive and well.

Ned went back to work along the Green River near Charcoal Bottom, helping several men, including Billy Tittsworth, round up wild horses, which they broke and sold as saddle and pack horses. While there he met a Shoshone woman called Tickup.

Tickup and her nine-year-old daughter, Mincy, were soon enamored with Ned. Mincy, of mixed Caucasian-Indian ancestry, looked up to Ned as a father figure, and Ned grew attached to the youngster. Tickup had left her husband, a Ute named Pony Beater, because he beat her and Mincy when he drank too much.

Pony Beater wanted his family back. When he came to get them, he forced Tickup to tie up Ned and he took his things. The Ute got drunk to celebrate, beat Tickup and Mincy, then fell asleep. Tickup slit Pony Beater's throat with a butcher knife. She took his belongings, and Ned's, too, and fled to be with her own people in Idaho.

Friends untied Ned, who hurried to find Tickup. By the time he located her, she was already living with a Shoshone man. In an ensuing fight, Ned lost all of his left ear except the bottom part holding the lobe. Tickup had sliced it off with a stone ax.

In revenge, Ned and his friends stole some ponies from the Shoshones. Unbeknownst to them, some of the ponies belonged to Sioux camped nearby. The Sioux followed the men, but their pursuit was interrupted by a group of Texas cowhands trailing a herd across the country. This probably prevented further bloodshed.

Ned took up with bad companions who became known as the Tip Gault gang. In addition to Ned and Tip Gault, other members of the gang included Jack Leath, Joe Pease, a man known only as Terresa, and Terresa's brother Casimero. The gang came to Carbon County in 1875 as part of a plan to illegally acquire horses.

Casimero and a new member of the group, Johnny Simo, went scouting for the Anderson horse herd which was being trailed across the country from California. They located the herd near Pass Creek, north of present-day Saratoga, and stampeded it, planning to round up the strays.

Meanwhile, back at the outlaw camp things were calm, so Ned traveled to Fort Steele for supplies. While killing time in the telegraph office there, he overheard a message coming over the wires from Fort Bridger. Ned knew Morse code and realized that the message told of the deaths of Casimero and Simo in a fracas over the Anderson horse herd.

Ned returned to the outlaw camp, and the Tip Gault gang plotted revenge for the deaths of their fellow rustlers by planning to steal as many horses as they could from the herd. They followed the herd eastward for four days, but the open terrain hampered their efforts.

Finally they succeeded in stampeding the herd with the accidental help of one of the horses from the herd itself. The horse had been spooked and ran into the midst of the gang members who took advantage of its fright by turning it back toward the other horses and stirring up the herd. During the ruckus, Joe Pease was badly injured, but the gang rustled some of the horses away from the herd and returned to their camp.

Seven of the stolen horses belonged to local rancher Bill Hawley. Hawley, a former Carbon County sheriff, owned the Hat Ranch on Pass Creek. He led a posse of his cowboys twenty miles to the outlaw camp to recover the stolen stock.

The Hawley men spotted the camp, but noting that only Ned Huddleston and the injured Joe Pease were in camp, they awaited the return of the rest of the gang. When the outlaws returned to camp, the posse patiently waited for the cover of darkness.

Then, in the flickering light of the campfire, Hawley's men shot the gang members. Tip Gault, who had earned a reputation as "King

Isom Dart. (Courtesy Denver Public Library, Western History Department)

of the Bitter Creek Thieves," and Terresa were killed. Jack Leath was wounded and tried to escape on horseback. He didn't travel far before he and his horse were both killed. Eventually all the members of the Tip Gault gang were killed, except for one. Ned Huddleston survived.

And the story of his survival during this attack is remarkable.

Joe Pease, severely hurt during the stampede, had suffered a broken jaw and a crushed chest. Ned had remained in camp with Pease when the other outlaws rode out. Ned's Civil War experiences, assisting a group of Confederate soldiers as their orderly, cook and nurse, helped him to make Pease comfortable; Ned probably provided some swigs of whiskey to ease his pain. But as nightfall approached, Pease died.

Ned walked out a short distance from camp to dig a grave, and it was while he was digging that Hawley and his men made their attack. Ned Huddleston avoided death by jumping into Joe Pease's grave. He spent the night there. When he was sure it was safe, he climbed from the grave, took the money belts from the dead men and left on foot. His deceased partners provided enough money to make Ned wealthy.

Even so, he tried to steal a horse from a nearby ranch, but the owner shot him twice, wounding him severely. Ned hobbled away and collapsed on the Overland Stage Road.

Coincidentally, he was discovered there by his old friend W. G. (Billy) Tittsworth. Tittsworth helped restore Ned to good health. Perhaps this brush with death and the reunion with his childhood friend convinced him to go straight. He changed his name to Isom (sometimes written as Isam or Isham) Dart. He moved to Oklahoma to make a new start and spent several years raising cotton on leased land there.

In Oklahoma, another chapter of Isom Dart's life overlapped with an earlier event. Dart arranged to bring Tickup and Mincy to the state. He paid tuition for Mincy to attend boarding school there.

In the mid-1880s, Tickup died of smallpox. Not long after, Dart and Mincy met a man named Madison M. (Matt) Rash. Rash took a liking to Mincy, and they traveled west together. Isom Dart didn't trust Rash, and he followed. By the time Rash arrived in Trinidad, Colorado, Mincy was no longer with him. Burroughs, in his history, speculates that Mincy probably developed the symptoms of the small pox which had claimed her mother and that Rash abandoned her.

Burroughs wrote that Dart had tracked the couple through the Oklahoma Territory but lost their trail. He continued on to the Brown's Park area of Wyoming, Colorado, and Utah. Coincidence again played a role in Dart's life. Matt Rash and Isom Dart both signed on to work at the Middlesex Land and Cattle Company, owned by the Bassett family.

During this period of his life, Dart again turned to "thieving," this time cattle rustling. He never sought revenge against Matt Rash, who had taken his beloved Mincy. Burroughs speculates that his upbringing as a slave taught Dart subservience, and therefore he did not punish Rash.

However, Charles Kelly, in *The Outlaw Trail*, gave a slightly different view of Ned's reluctance to avenge Mincy's disappearance. He wrote that, "Rash told such a plausible story that the Negro decided not to kill him, at least for the present."

Along with Angus McDougal, Jim McKnight and others, Dart and Matt Rash composed an outlaw group known as the "Bassett gang." Devoted followers of Elizabeth Bassett, a woman with a sick husband and five small children, the gang mostly stuck to cattle and horse rustling.

The gang burned one of Henry Hoy's buildings one night and Angus McDougal and Isom Dart were jailed in the Routt County jail in Hahn's Peak, Colorado, for the offense. Dart broke out of jail and left the country. McDougal was sentenced to the Colorado State Penitentiary.

A warrant was later issued for Dart's arrest on charges of livestock theft in Sweetwater County, Wyoming. The sheriff deputized Joe Philbrick, considered one of the toughest men in Rock Springs, so he could bring Dart in.

Philbrick located Dart and took him into custody, but on the trip back to Rock Springs, the buckboard and team went off the road into a draw. The deputy was injured, but Dart was not hurt.

He could have escaped there and then. If he'd been just any western outlaw, he might have. But this was Isom Dart, who exhibited some good qualities along with the bad ones.

Dart helped the deputy, calmed the horses, and righted the wagon, which he drove into Rock Springs. He dropped the deputy off at the hospital and returned the horses and wagon to the livery stable. Then, Isom Dart turned himself in at the town jail.

Philbrick later testified to Dart's kindness and integrity, and Dart went free.

Dart earned several nicknames, including "Tan-Mex," "Quick-Shot," and "the Old Black Fox." He was arrested several other times for livestock theft, but the charges never seemed to stick. Supposedly, the cattle in Dart's personal herd were acquired honestly.

However, he had all three characters of his brand, the "I D Bar," welded to a single, short shaft. The shaft could be concealed in Dart's slicker, which he carried tied behind the cantle of his saddle.

Dart taught the Bassett children, including the daughter who would eventually become known as Queen Ann, cowboy skills, like how to use the lariat. He enjoyed spending time with children.

Burroughs wrote, "Such was Isom's gusto for life, however, his physical and nervous constitution, he everlastingly had to be up and doing. No man ever loved activity more; and few possessed greater physical strength."

Dart stood six-feet-two-inches tall. His chest measured forty-six inches and his waist measured thirty-two inches. His physical strength no doubt helped him earn his reputation as an excellent all-around cowman. And though Isom Dart never participated in a rodeo, except for his early work as a clown, he was considered a peerless rider of bucking broncs.

But Dart's destiny led him into the path of another well-known Wyoming figure. The Old Black Fox would not outsmart the hired killer's rifle.

Tom Horn, the infamous stock detective, came to Brown's Park in 1900. Horn posed as a rancher and horse buyer, using an assumed name. Matt Rash, who had bought a ranch of his own, hired Horn to help with the roundup. One day Rash and Horn found Dart butchering a bull which was clearly branded with someone else's brand. An argument ensued between Rash and Dart. It evolved into a heated discussion of past cattle rustling ventures in which Rash and Dash were partners. Horn listened and said little.

Horn disappeared after that, but warnings were found posted to cabin doors throughout the area. The warnings threatened rustlers to quit their illegal operations or leave within thirty days.

Some people did leave the area, but Rash and Dart remained. Matt Rash was shot and killed while eating his lunch on July 8, 1900, in his cabin on Cold Spring Mountain. Dart was killed October 3, 1900, as he came from his Summit Spring cabin on Cold Spring Mountain. The fifty-one-year-old died from a bullet shot from a Winchester .30–.30 rifle thought to belong to Tom Horn.

Tom Horn was never arrested for the murders of Matt Rash and Isom Dart, however, three years later he was convicted of murdering fourteen-year-old Willie Nickell in southeastern Wyoming. He died by hanging on November 20, 1903, in Cheyenne.

Erhard, in the article in the *Rock Springs Rocket,* states that Dart possessed an "engaging personality," which allowed him to leave "an ineffaceable imprint in many minds both for his daring deeds and his unswerving integrity."

Historian Cary Stiff summarized in the *Denver Post Empire Magazine* that Dart was one of the few black men in Colorado's history to pursue a cattle rustling career. He writes, arguably, "But more important than how he lived was how he died—at the hands of none other than Tom Horn, one of the West's most infamous hired killers."

Taylor Pennock

TAYLOR PENNOCK, ONE of the earliest residents of the Platte Valley area, served as a guide and scout, guiding hunting expeditions for General George Crook, among others. He held a variety of jobs during his exciting life, including those of bartender, gold miner, and hotel owner.

Many of Pennock's memories were chronicled in the 1929 *Annals of Wyoming*, as told to I. R. Conniss (probably I. M. Conness) of Rawlins and Saratoga. Pennock recalled many of his experiences and provided a picture of what life was like in the Platte Valley during the late 1800s.

Pennock was one of the first men to explore the Medicine Bow mountains, hunting game and exploring for minerals. He probably sharpened his survival skills during the Civil War, when he was captured and held as a prisoner of war by the Confederate forces. Pennock served in the Sixteenth Regiment of Illinois Volunteer Cavalry. He enlisted in December 1862 and was discharged in the early summer months of 1865. His term of service had not been an easy one.

For more than a year before the end of the war, Pennock suffered in Andersonville and other Confederate prisons. He was captured by Confederate soldiers at Jonesville, Virginia, on January 3, 1864.

For three weeks the prisoners were confined at Scott's prison in Richmond, Virginia, located near Libby prison. The next six weeks were spent on Bell Island in the James River, and then prisoners were sent to Andersonville Prison. They were kept there for eleven months.

In "The Recollections of Taylor Pennock," Pennock recalled being transferred to Savannah when General Stoneman raided

Macon, Georgia. The prisoners were moved to the Melon Stockade when Union forces attacked Savannah.

"We were there for six weeks. When we left Melon, we ate rutabagas for breakfast and were on the train two days and nights without anything more to eat," Pennock stated.

The prisoners slept in an open coal car, suffering through sleet and rainy weather. They received a half-pound of shelled corn each when they arrived at Thomasville, Georgia, and then marched sixty-three miles to Albany, Georgia.

Freedom came on April 29, 1865, after the surrender of General Robert E. Lee.

Pennock returned to Illinois but didn't like it there after the war because it was "too tame." He found a job as a teamster, freighting corn and onions from Fort Leavenworth, Kansas, to Denver, Colorado.

He spent the winter of 1865 in Fort Kearny, Nebraska, on the Wood River. Pennock traded bread, flour, and other staples to Indians there, receiving furs and moccasins in return. He trapped beavers for beaver pelts. He remembered that about six hundred Pawnee Indians stayed in one camp and said they "treated me fine."

Pennock traveled west, obtaining a government contract to set ten thousand telegraph poles along the old government road, the transcontinental route that preceded the Union Pacific Railroad.

After returning to Illinois and Denver, the frontier West beckoned Pennock yet again. In 1872 he came to Fort Steele. He hunted game for the Union Pacific tie camp on Rock Creek, taking three or four head per week to feed the 150 men stationed there. He recalled elk herds ranging from thirty to two hundred in number. Antelope herds had "thirty to one thousand in them and were scattered all over the open country." Pennock saw ten thousand elk in one herd in early November.

In 1872, few people resided at Fort Steele. The first tie camp began in 1868; Coe and Carter's tie camp north of Brush Creek started in winter of 1872. Tom Sun, another Carbon County pioneer, worked cutting ties on French Creek with several Frenchmen there.

Pennock told of Indians making a run on the tie drive at the mouth of Brush Creek in 1873. They later attacked the tie drive at the Platte River Crossing on the Overland Trail, he said. The Indians

Back row, left, John Sullivan and Taylor Pennock. (Sullivan was his half brother.) Front row, left, is Adelaide Young Sullivan, and Rosy Rudersdorf Pennock. (Courtesy Saratoga Historical and Cultural Association)

wanted horses, but the frightened animals ran into the camp, foiling their efforts.

Pennock freighted supplies to the Coe and Carter tie camp that winter and spring, then went to Fort Steele with the tie drive. He helped take the ties from the river at Fort Steele and load them on railroad cars for the Union Pacific. He also trapped with Ed Alley, catching beaver, mink, and coyotes.

Pennock said that thousands of beaver lived at the head of Cow Creek near the timber. In the first three weeks, the men caught 120 beaver. There were no ranches in the Platte Valley at that time.

The trappers built cabins on the site where the Huston ranch stands today. Pennock said that the Indians in the area were peaceful, and although the Utes came to hunt, they did not cause any trouble.

The men trapped until the streams froze and then hunted game for soldiers at Fort Steele, drying the meat when winter caused them to be snowbound.

Pennock then moved from the mountains to the riverbanks, staying at Bennett's Ferry. He said that he located one mile below the houses on the McFarlane Ranch and six miles above the old Overland Crossing where the emigrants crossed when the water within the fort's reservation was too high for safety.

While he lived near the ferry, Pennock killed antelope and sold them for one dollar each to emigrants who were crossing the North Platte. During those years, the ferry was operated by using a cable made of rope.

Pennock seemed restless, moving around a lot and trying a variety of jobs. During the late 1800s, men did what they had to do to eke out a living, and many of them worked at several different occupations.

Pennock tried mining after his stay at the ferry, purchasing mining claims in the Seminoe Mountains. He had freighted supplies into the mill there for a couple of months previously so he was familiar with the area. But he soon decided mining was not for him. The hostilities of the Indians in the area undoubtedly contributed to his decision.

Pennock spent the winter in the isolation of the Freezeout Mountains, east of the Seminoes, trapping for beaver again. He said, "I never saw a single person nor any horses or cattle except one wild horse."

Pennock's diverse jobs included working in Tom Ryan's dairy near Saratoga and operating a hotel for a short time at Fort Steele. A year after he sold the hotel, which he had built, it burned down. The spring of 1876 found Pennock serving as a bartender for J.W. Hugus, who was the post sutler at Fort Steele at the time.

After his marriage to Rose Rudersdorf on May 27, 1877, Pennock took up a large homestead near Saratoga, east of the river. In 1988, a descendant of the Pennock family placed the Pennock homestead and freighting quarters "almost immediately northwest of the stone gates on the Pick Pike road toward Old Baldy Club and Cedar Creek." The Pennocks had two sons, Frank and Edwin.

The December 12, 1895, issue of the *Saratoga Sun* reported that Pennock, working as the foreman for the Pass Creek Company, had left with Ed Ringer to oversee the company's property on the Red Desert, where sheep often grazed during the winters.

Pennock guided several expeditions of military men who wanted to hunt in the mountains. Events that transpired on one of those trips probably saved him from being killed in what was then known as the Meeker Massacre.

He guided General Crook's hunting party in 1879, which included Webb Hayes, Major Thornburgh, and Dr. Draper. Pennock reported that Battle Creek held lots of fish, the native brook trout weighing about three-quarters of a pound each. The hunters also saw three bears in one day, he said. "One very fine deer" that they killed was sent to Webb's father, President Rutherford B. Hayes, who had it mounted.

Pennock also led hunting expeditions for Generals Marcy and Whipple, along with several more for General Crook.

Later that fall, Pennock guided Thornburgh's brother and two bankers from Tennessee on a hunt. This expedition left Fort Steele for Battle Lake on the same day that Major Thornburgh left Rawlins for the White River Agency. Thornburgh was summoned to take troops from Fort Steele to the White River Agency to settle the problems that had arisen between Ute Indians and Agent Nathan Meeker.

Although the major wanted Pennock to serve as his guide, his brother insisted that Pennock guide the hunters instead. Thornburgh and Meeker were killed in the resulting battle at the White River Agency, and both sides suffered heavy losses. Pennock's party learned of the massacre shortly after and discontinued their hunt.

Pennock recalled that after they returned to Fort Steele, he hauled two loads of freight, driving four-horse teams, for J. W. Hugus to the White River Agency. The freighter traveled with military escorts through the area where the battle had taken place. Along the way, they saw freighters who had not been so lucky. The road was littered with the destroyed wagons of freighters who had been killed.

Pennock said that he camped a few hundred yards below the Milk Creek battlegrounds, and although the dead had been buried, slaughtered horses still lay on the ground. The group stayed in tents for the three weeks they spent at the White River Agency because all the other shelters had been destroyed.

Pennock recalled that prior to that battle, the Indians had driven game from the Sierra Madre Mountains by setting forest fires.

🥨🥨

It seems only fitting that a man who spent so much of his time in the mountains should receive the honor of having a mountain bear his name. In 1928, the U. S. Forest Service, in conjunction with the National Geographic Board, renamed a mountain northeast of Saratoga, calling it Pennock Mountain. The mountain had formerly been known as Wood Mountain or Cedar Mountain.

The renaming was done to avoid duplication of names in the Medicine Bow and Hayden Forests, according to the *Saratoga Sun,* which reported the name change in its December 6, 1928, issue.

At the same time that Pennock Mountain was christened with its new moniker, Bald Mountain—more commonly known as Mount Baldy—was renamed Kennaday Peak in honor of the late Andrew J. ("Jack") Kennaday, who had been a forest ranger and pioneer resident in the Cedar Creek area.

Pennock died in 1932 while on an afternoon excursion with his wife. The June 16, 1932, *Saratoga Sun* carried the news of the pioneer's death, saying that Pennock collapsed while driving the couple's car, "expiring in the arms of his wife."

Pennock had spent sixty years in Carbon County and was an active member of the community. He was a member of the local Masonic order and of the American Legion.

The newspaper reported, "Local business houses were closed during the funeral, which was one of the largest ever seen here."

Bonaparte Napoleon "Boney" Earnest

Boney Earnest counted Taylor Pennock among his friends, a group which included some of the most famous characters in the legends of the Wild West—Buffalo Bill Cody, Calamity Jane, and Wild Bill Hickok.

The *Wyoming Tribune-Leader* called Earnest "a western character of the truest type, one for whom life was a great adventure."

Earnest became an Indian scout and government guide at Fort Steele, arriving in Rawlins in 1868. Contractors were just beginning work on the railroad grade between the military post and Rawlins.

Named for Napoleon Bonaparte, "Boney" as he came to be known, left Toronto, Canada, in 1864 traveling to Kansas. He joined a group going to the Great Salt Lake, using a route that took them through Fort Laramie, Wyoming Territory. It was the young Canadian's first experience in Wyoming, the state where he would choose to spend the greater part of his life.

Soon Boney was associated with the Butterfield Stage Company. He helped survey a trail from Atchison, Kansas, to Denver, Colorado, with points in Topeka and Salina, Kansas. It was a dangerous time in the West, with Indians trying to protect their land from the flood of emigrants who traversed it regularly. Four hundred soldiers protected the survey party as they plotted the route.

Boney met Buffalo Bill at Salt Creek, north of Fort Leavenworth, Kansas. The two men crossed the plains together, arriving in Cheyenne Wells, Colorado, in 1865.

Boney quit the stage business and bought a ranch, but in the fall of 1868, he sold the ranch and traveled further west. He worked again in the transportation business, this time for the Union Pacific while the construction of the transcontinental railroad took place in southern Wyoming.

His travels eventually brought him to the North Platte crossing west of Laramie City and near present-day Saratoga, where his brother, Frank, was helping Ed Bennett operate the ferry. Boney stayed in the region for most of the rest of his life.

Boney took a sub-contract with a man named Thomas de Soleil (Tom Sun), a French Canadian, with Sprague, Davis, and Company to set up a logging camp in 1868. The crew of about a dozen men became known as the "French Crew," and the logs they cut for railroad ties were the first ones to float down the river to Fort Steele. The creek where they worked soon became known as French Creek.

Gay Day Alcorn, in her book, *Tough Country,* called Sun and Boney Earnest "two of Wyoming's most important pioneers."

A talented hunter, Boney often accompanied visiting members of the nobility on hunts. He was reported to have been among the group of hunters that killed one of the last buffalo in central Wyoming.

The gold rush beckoned him further west, though. Boney searched for the precious metal in the Atlantic City-South Pass region of Fremont County, Wyoming, but he didn't find any claims he felt held promise.

Boney secured a map from "Uncle Bob" Foote, a resident of Fort Halleck, who had traveled over the Fort Halleck trail to Fort Washakie and knew the South Pass area. The route ran four miles north of where Parco was later located (now Sinclair), then west to Whiskey Gap and the Sweetwater River.

Boney said, "There were no important events occurring on our route except that we saw two small parties of Indians, one at Split Rock and one at Rocky Ridge, but they never attacked us and we just called honors even."

When the group arrived safely at South Pass, Boney was "amazed with the prospects." It didn't take him very long to change his mind. After about a week, he came to the conclusion "that all that glittered was not gold."

He recalled his trip to South Pass, Wyoming, in Ruth Beebe's book, *Reminiscing on the Sweetwater.* None of Boney's party, which included five other miners, knew the terrain. Indians were considered extremely dangerous at the time. However, while at South Pass City he heard tales of gold in California, so he headed out to California to seek his fortune.

California's gold lost its luster when Boney heard that San Francisco had been "swallowed up by an earthquake." He turned back to Wyoming.

In 1872, he returned to Rawlins and joined Tom Sun in forming a joint stock company. Their business included trapping, hunting, and prospecting for precious metals like gold and silver. At the time, the men also scouted for the government and fought Indians.

Boney stated, "This kind of life was not very remunerative, but always pleasant and exciting." One of the exciting incidents in his life revolved around an Indian battle near Fort Steele.

In 1874, Boney helped Yank Sullivan, a recently discharged soldier, build a ranch about three miles down the river from Fort Steele. Before the men could climb out of bed one morning, they heard a war whoop. Two hundred Indians surrounded the site. Boney's experience, the last Indian fight he participated in, was recorded in a manuscript by Rose Roybal as part of the Works Project Administration file at the Wyoming State Archives. The manuscript quotes a letter that Earnest wrote to the *Rawlins Republican*, in June 9, 1927.

"In less time than it takes to tell it," the pioneer said, "we both grabbed our guns and were in action as we slept with our guns." Boney stated that both sides "were badly embarrassed by the tall sage brush," during the gunfire that followed. He credited the sagebrush with saving his and Sullivan's lives, though, because the Indians left them alone and directly attacked Fort Steele.

News of the attack on the military post flooded the telegraph wires and soon the Rawlins Rangers mobilized a force of twenty-five men. The men traveled to the area that would later become Parco, where the Indians had injured one of the section men of the railroad.

In an incident which would cause Mark Twain to laugh, five civilians and twenty soldiers formed a party to bury Boney and Sullivan, who they thought had died in the skirmish. But, to paraphrase Twain, rumors of their deaths had been exaggerated.

"It's needless to say that they were all surprised to find us alive," Boney recalled.

Sun and Earnest dissolved their joint stock company in 1877, "calling honors even." The two men went into the cattle ranching business. The Sun Ranch was located at Devil's Gate, where it exists today. Boney located his ranch near the mouth of the Sweetwater River.

Boney married Martha Canzada Brantley, often called Canzada or "Aunt Mattie," on November 9, 1881. According to Beebe, Martha, who hailed from Tennessee, is classified as one of Wyoming's "original settlers" who "had an even more colorful life than her husband."

After her parents died, the future Mrs. Earnest had traveled to Denver and lived with the J. B. Pierson family. She traveled with them to Deadwood, South Dakota, to search for gold, but then went to Texas in 1877 to stay with her sister.

Beebe recounted the story of Martha's trip to Texas.

She wrote, "In spite of warnings of Indians on the warpath, and road agents holding up the stage coaches, she took off." Beebe stated that Martha had three thousand dollars in gold sewed in her petticoats and two dollars in her purse. When road agents held up the stagecoach, they ordered the passengers out. Martha began to cry and asked the robbers if they were so mean that they'd take the last two dollars of a poor girl.

Beebe wrote, "They gave her money back and five dollars besides!"

According to Alcorn, in 1883, the Sand Creek Land and Cattle Company, Limited, a British company, purchased Boney's ranch and that of his brother, Frank, for $106,000. The purchase price included the log buildings, equipment, 2,800 head of cattle and fifty horses, and all the water rights. Boney became the foreman and Frank served as manager. The ranch headquarters located at Bennett's Ferry later became known as the Pick Ranch, and the British company ceased its operations of the ranch in 1897.

During this time, Boney found the body of Charles Strong, a hunter who was murdered along with his companion Morris Waln while on a hunting trip in the area. The men, Strong from New York City and Waln from Pennsylvania, took their trip in 1888.

The mystery of the murders of the men was never solved, but Beebe wrote that the Waln family hired Pinkerton detectives who

Martha and Boney Earnest. (Courtesy Carbon County Museum)

identified a suspect who was already serving a life sentence in Colorado for another crime. A monument was erected in memory of Morris Waln and stands on the Hank Miles' original homestead.

When the Pathfinder Dam was built in 1908, Boney lost the ranch he owned then, but he said, "Uncle Sam paid me a good price for putting me out of business."

Years later, after the construction of the Pathfinder Dam, the Earnests made their home at Alcova, in Natrona County. They took logs from their original ranch home and placed them into their new one. They celebrated their fiftieth wedding anniversary at Alcova in 1931.

Boney died there in 1933 of pneumonia at the age of eighty-seven. Boney had loved to tell stories, and the *Saratoga Sun* report of his death stated, "His many thrilling and colorful experiences had provided him with a great store of western lore, and his genial companionship was sought by scores who enjoyed his stories."

The *Casper Tribune-Herald* reported "Aunt Mattie's" ninety-sixth birthday in 1948, mentioning the hospitality of the Earnests at their Alcova ranch which served as a "halfway point for travelers between Casper and Rawlins." She died the next year, in early June 1949, at the age of ninety-seven.

Richard & Margaret Savage

OTHER CANADIANS WHO came to Wyoming to settle in the area now known as Carbon County included Richard and Margaret Savage. Their story not only demonstrates the hardships endured by the first people making their homes in the area, but it contains at its heart an elegant expression of a deep and romantic love.

Richard Savage came to Carbon County in 1868 to trap and hunt game for the government. He was the first man to import Oxford (black-faced) sheep from Canada, and also the first, according to the *Rawlins Republican,* to experiment with crossing buffalo and cattle. The paper stated that his experiment was successful, and that Savage had a whole herd of quarter-breeds.

He was born in Niagara Falls, Canada, and traveled west with his brother. Savage hunted with Boney Earnest, E. W. (Ed) Bennett, and Sandy Preay, earning a reputation as a "wonder of wonders" with his black powder rifle, according to Alcorn's *Tough Country.*

Alcorn reported that during one hunting trip with the men, Preay was left in charge of the camp and hunting cabin while the others traveled to Fort Steele. When they arrived, they learned that Preay had been killed by Indians. The hunters returned to their camp, quietly inspecting the area. None of them wanted to look into the cabin to see if killers still lurked there, so they drew lots.

Richard Savage earned the privilege. He peered into the cabin and was startled by his friend Preay asking who was there. Preay hadn't seen anyone near the camp since the men had left for the fort.

Like several others from his era, Savage became acquainted with men and women destined to become western legends—Jim Baker, Calamity Jane, and Buffalo Bill Cody.

Richard Savage. (Courtesy Saratoga Historical & Cultural Association)

Savage returned to Canada to go into the lumber business, a family operation. While there, he met Margaret Ann Watson, a young woman of Scottish descent. He talked continuously about a beautiful place called Wyoming Territory and said he longed to go back.

Their romance blossomed, and they were married. Margaret eventually agreed to go see this wondrous land that had her husband so enthralled. Their daughter Pearl was born in Canada in 1879. Pearl's twin brother died ten days after his birth.

According to Alcorn, Richard came back to Wyoming Territory first and Margaret came later, in 1881. When she stepped off the train, her beauty struck many of the men speechless.

Margaret didn't know how strong her pioneer heart would have to be. She would not see another woman until nine months after her arrival.

Margaret's father came to see the couple. His opinion was that the wildly beautiful, but barren, Wyoming Territory was no

The Savages' stone home. (Courtesy Saratoga Historical & Cultural Association)

place for a lady. He offered his daughter the opportunity to return to Canada.

Margaret stayed with Richard.

Her father, tasting defeat, decided to send her several items to make her lonely life in the wilds of the territory more comfortable. He built a wooden dresser for her, which is displayed now at the Saratoga Museum in Saratoga, Wyoming.

But her husband decided to make his beautiful and loyal wife more comfortable, too. Realizing that Wyoming Territory was nothing like the life she was accustomed to, Richard set about changing that. His family had also known the finer things of life. Richard's eldest brother was christened at St. Paul's Cathedral in London, the same church where Prince Charles and Lady Diana Spencer, many years later, spoke their ill-fated wedding vows.

Richard built Margaret a mansion. And not just any mansion, but an opulent, fabulous home of stone. The elegant house was built in 1891, and it still stands on private property owned by Burton Tuttle. The house can still stir images of romance, for though the floral wallpaper is faded and the woodwork is aging, the quiet rooms show the elegance Richard hoped to recreate for his wife.

The stones were quarried on the ranch, leftovers from a rejected railroad project. Charles Francis Adams, a grandson of President Adams, in 1887, decided to build a railroad line from Saratoga to Brush Creek and on to Walden, Colorado, with a spur traveling to Aspen, Colorado. In 1889, Burlington Northern took over, quarrying the stones along the river near the location of the Savage house. The stones were to be used to build a stone bridge for the railroad. But the project was rejected, and Richard Savage hauled the stones, already cut, to build his mansion.

Alcorn said that the rooms were once filled with fine furniture, and the Savages were served by employees wearing black uniforms with white aprons. The woodwork in the Savage House was classic.

Rose gardens trimmed the outside of the house, and a room with a three-sided window graced the home. In 1894, Richard added a carriage house, built from materials he purchased from Fort Steele when the barracks were torn down there.

The Savages built a substantial herd of sheep from stock imported from their Canadian homeland. The stone home was headquarters for the Savage Sheep Company.

The Savages had five daughters. Their youngest, Irene, wrote her name in the wet cement of one of steps leading into the house where it remains today. Another daughter, Daisy Wyland, told a story of her mother in the *Rawlins Republican* article which celebrated Richard's ninety-eighth birthday in July 1939. According to Wyland, Indians still roamed the area when her mother arrived. She recalled that when Mr. Savage was away from home, Mrs. Savage often sat up all night with a rifle across her lap because she thought she heard Indians outside. On one of these all-night vigils, she discovered that the frightening sounds were horses racing around the house.

Alcorn's book contains another story about Margaret Savage's fear of Indians. The Savage family apparently heard that Indians in their area had gone on a rampage. Mrs. Savage and her daughters stayed in the store at Fort Steele, carefully studying and shopping among all the

Margaret Savage. (Courtesy Saratoga Historical & Cultural Association)

merchandise there until the false rumor was dispelled. Fenimore
Chatterton, the post sutler at the time, entertained them at the store.
Chatterton later became Governor of Wyoming. The Savage women,
safe and unharmed, returned home none the worse for wear.

The daughters of Richard and Margaret were: Georgiana (Mrs.
Robert L.) Fowler of Winnetka, IL; Gladys (Mrs. Andrew J.) Wright
of Plainfield, NJ; Irene (Mrs. Brenton) Van Cleave of St. Louis,
MO; Miss Pearl Savage of Salt Lake City; and Margaret (Mrs. Roy)
"Daisy" Wyland who lived on the Savage Ranch along the Platte
River. All of the daughters are now deceased.

Alcorn said that the Savage daughters enjoyed playing mischie-
vous pranks on their tutors, including tormenting one governess by
hiding a badger skin under the bed, tied to a string, so they could
scare her with it.

The young women were educated in Saratoga, at Fort Steele,
and in Salt Lake City, Utah. Alcorn said that the Savage girls later

traveled to Washington, D. C., where they were entertained at the White House.

Richard Savage said in the *Rawlins Republican* article that he remembered buying his first buffalo bull in 1894 for three hundred dollars. The bull was shot and killed some time later "by a zealous hunter." Supposedly, the bull was the last buffalo in Carbon County.

In September 1897, Richard Savage moved his family to Salt Lake City, Utah. He commuted between Utah and Wyoming after that, and he still owned his Wyoming ranch when he turned ninety-eight. Margaret Savage died in 1918 and, according to the *Saratoga Sun*, "[Pearl] took over the running of the family home and reared her sisters." Pearl lived to be one-hundred-years old.

A sheep wagon, commemorating the Savages' contribution to the Wyoming sheep industry, stands on the grounds at the Saratoga Museum, and Margaret Savage's wedding dress is displayed there as well. The wedding dress is black, created in the very elegant style of the day.

The ranch remained in the Savage family until 1962, and the stone house stands as a silent reminder of a tender romance that grew strong in the lonely, barren territory.

"Life's a good thing," Richard Savage stated in the *Rawlins Republican* article commemorating his ninety-eighth birthday, "but it's too short." He died in 1939.

Henry Seton-Karr

MANY ENGLISHMEN CAME to Wyoming to hunt in the late 1800s, and some of them became so enthralled with the country that they returned. Henry Seton-Karr even purchased a ranch, known today as the Pick Ranch.

Local historian Gay Day Alcorn traveled to England to research the English gentleman who made part of Carbon County's history through his organization of the ranch. Much of the information in this profile comes from her thoroughly-researched and authoritative book, *Tough Country*.

Seton-Karr, an Oxford graduate, became the largest stockholder in the British-owned Sand Creek Land and Cattle Company, Limited, which was organized in 1883. He also served as managing director and secretary for the company, which kept an office in London, England.

Other stockholders included his family, friends, and business associates. According to Alcorn, the ranch grew out of Seton-Karr's cattle partnership with Frank Earnest at Warm Springs (later known as Saratoga). Earnest and his brother Boney, along with the "wild and woolly cowboy foreman" Clabe Young were the only local men holding stock.

The adventure all began with Seton-Karr's love of hunting. In 1875, on a hunting trip to Norway during his Oxford days, the Englishman bagged a red-deer stag. When he returned the next year, he saw a set of elk antlers from America in the gunmakers' shop. This sight inspired him to travel to America to hunt.

On the recommendation of another English hunter, Seton-Karr chose Frank Earnest as his guide.

Crossing the Atlantic Ocean, Seton-Karr and Thomas Bate, a fellow hunter, were passengers on the *White Star,* a German luxury liner. Transportation in the region that would become Carbon County, Wyoming, consisted of stagecoaches, wagons, horses, and trains. It was quite a contrast for young Englishmen coming to hunt. It truly must have seemed like "tough country" to them when they arrived at Fort Steele via the transcontinental locomotive.

Earnest met them at the train and organized the hunting group, which also included Jack Roberts, another hunter, and Bill Perkins. Perkins drove the supply wagon and served as the expedition's cook. Alcorn related the following humorous incident about Bill's cooking.

She wrote, "Bill's cooking was extremely poor. Seton-Karr decided to help him out by giving him a cookbook brought from England. This offer infuriated Bill. With a loud burst of profanity the cook threw the book into the nearest sagebrush. Seton-Karr decided it was probably all right as the camp was short of eggs and every recipe began, 'Take so many eggs.'"

The men managed to survive on whatever meals Bill whipped up, however, because they bagged not only elk (which the English called "wapiti") but antelope, black-tail deer, and buffalo on the trip. They also killed one grizzly bear, a big-horn ram, and a lynx. The four-month trip took them from Fort Steele to Whiskey Gap, the Jack Creek area, and Grand Encampment. The hunters even met Jim Baker, the famous mountain man and trapper, while they traveled through the Snake River area.

Alcorn wrote, "Seton-Karr concluded, 'From start to finish our four months' trip was a glorious kind of school-boy picnic,...the pleasant flavour of which has never faded from my mind.'"

Seton-Karr's first hunting adventure in the American West and the wilds of Wyoming was so successful, in fact, that he made the event an annual excursion. He became good friends with Earnest and said that Earnest did "his level best to show sport to two raw British 'tender-foots' who had employed him to that end...."

In the summer of 1883, Seton-Karr purchased two thousand head of cattle with Frank Earnest. The cattle were shipped from Utah to Rawlins, and Alcorn wrote that the "cowboys met the train with lariats and branding irons."

Frank Earnest's brand, a pick with a bar added, became their brand. The ranch gained the nickname the Pick Ranch. The nickname stuck. The bridge that crosses the North Platte River on the ranch property became known as the Pick Bridge as well.

The Sand Creek Land and Cattle Company, Limited, filed Articles of Association with the London Registrar of Companies, with 100,000 British pounds of capital and ten thousand shares of stock valued at ten pounds each. Seton-Karr held the majority of shares. The ranch secretary was Joseph Hugh Jefferson, an English aristocrat.

Alcorn wrote, "Seton-Karr was not new to the world of Western cattle companies, as he was also a major shareholder along with the Earl of Aberdeen and the Marquis of Tweeddale, in the Capitol Freehold Land and Investment Company, Ltd., better known as the XIT Ranch of Texas."

Both Frank and his brother, Boney Earnest, sold their ranches to the company, receiving $106,000 in return. Part of their payment was made in shares, and each of the brothers held 275 shares of stock in the new company. The company purchased all the water rights, 2,800 head of cattle, fifty horses, and the log buildings, and equipment from the Earnests.

Frank Earnest was chosen as manager, a position he held for five years, and Boney became a ranch foreman. The ranch, which included 150,000 acres of grazing rights on the Upper North Platte River on Canyon Creek and in Bates Hole, had its headquarters at Bennett's Ferry.

Alcorn wrote, "The large Pick operation had numerous cowboys, several foremen, a general manager, a secretary at the ranch, and a managing director-secretary in London." The secretary in Rawlins could contact the London office by wiring "Washakie" through the telegraph.

Of Seton-Karr, Alcorn wrote that he "cut a dashing figure for contemporaries on both sides of the Atlantic." He married Edith Eliza Pilkington, the daughter of a wealthy English industrialist.

In England, Seton-Karr's father-in-law suggested that he run for election to the House of Commons. He won as the Conservative candidate and represented the borough of St. Helen's. He continued to serve as a Member of Parliament for twenty-one years.

Seton-Karr also served his country during the Boer War, by organizing a sharpshooters' corps to serve at the front. He wrote a book, *The Call to Arms*, which chronicled his experience. Seton-Karr was knighted in 1902 by King Edward VII. The honor undoubtedly made him proud, as Seton-Karr's ancestry included Mary Seton, "an extremely close friend and confidant of the historic Mary Queen of Scots," according to Alcorn. The family had owned the Scottish estate, Kippilaw, since 1657, and Seton-Karr served as the estate's laird.

Seton-Karr also participated in the 1887 American Trophy Exhibition at Earl's Court in England. Members of the English Natural History Museum measured the exhibits, shown by many Englishmen who had hunted in the American West. Many of the exhibits included elk which had been killed in the mountainous areas of Carbon County.

Another book written by Seton-Karr was entitled, *My Sporting Holidays*, and it included photographs that he took with his own camera. The book was published in London.

The Sand Creek Land and Cattle Company, Limited, ceased operations in 1899 after beginning to wrap up its business in 1897. Alcorn wrote that the company, "like the other giants of the range cattle era, used lands which they could not claim, having deeds to little or nothing. Following the bust in the range cattle industry, trends were for much smaller units that could be utilized with maximum efficiency."

Another Englishman, Walter B. Cowan, purchased the ranch headquarters site and the Pick brand. He named it Deerwood Ranche and acquired other lands as they became available. He married Julia Smith in 1893.

Julia had previously been engaged to the ranch secretary, Joseph Hugh Jefferson. Walter Cowan died at age forty-one of a ruptured appendix, and Julia returned to England after the sale of the ranch. The ranch again became known as the Pick Ranch.

Henry Seton-Karr died when the *Empress of Ireland* sank in the St. Lawrence River during World War I.

Kenny Olson, who owned the ranch in 1999, said that Henry Seton-Karr's great grandson once visited the ranch that his ancestor began.

R.E.G. Huntington

JESUS CALLED TO HIS Apostles to be fishers of men. This might also apply to the life of Roswell Elbridge Gerry Huntington, Doctor of Divinity. Dr. Huntington's spiritual work was complemented by a hobby to which he was very devoted—fishing.

Though not much has been written about Dr. Huntington, his stamp upon Saratoga remains indelible.

The Cambridge University graduate came to Carbon County after working as a missionary in the West in the middle 1870s. His mission here was to serve the congregation of St. Thomas Episcopal Church in Rawlins, but he also served people in Saratoga. Dr. Huntington is credited with organizing the Episcopal Church of the Heavenly Rest in Saratoga.

The church, more than a century old, still stands today at 106 West Main Street, an admirable reminder of Dr. Huntington's work. It is known today as St. Barnabas Episcopal Church.

Dr. Huntington arrived in Rawlins in 1886, the rector of St. Thomas. The *Rawlins Daily Times,* in its special Saratoga Centennial Edition, reported that the Huntingtons were popular, "being a gracious intelligent family."

Dr. Huntington had married Miss Florence M. Rosewell on February 10, 1865, at Colton, New York. The couple had nine children: Gertrude, Laura, Frederick, Lucia, Arthur, Roberta, Carolyn, Florence Eleanor, and Albert. Though the family moved often, they tried to see to it that the children received good educations.

During his tenure in Rawlins, Dr. Huntington sometimes traveled the forty miles to Saratoga on horseback to hold Episcopal services there. The first Episcopal services were held in Saratoga on

The Reverend R.E.G. Huntington, Rector of St. Thomas Episcopal Church in Rawlins in 1886, is credited with starting Saratoga's Episcopal church, now known as St. Barnabas Episcopal Church. (Courtesy of Carbon County Museum)

May 1, 1888. According to local historian Alcorn, Saratoga was a stagecoach stop on the C. M. Scribner line from Encampment to Walcott Junction at the time.

In 1889, Huntington resigned from St. Thomas, accepting a new position at Saratoga. The church building now known as St. Barnabas in Saratoga was built by architect Thomas Hood, who also built the rectory. The rectory also remains as part of the church grounds today.

The first services in the little church were held in early 1889, with Bishop Ethelbert Talbot officiating, with assistance by Archdeacon Plant and Dr. Huntington.

The *Rawlins Daily Times* Saratoga Centennial Edition reported that "the building was in an incomplete state and the temperature was low." The congregation, though uncomfortable, reported that "the inconvenience was well worth it being impressed by both the structure and Reverend Huntington."

While the rectory was being built, the Huntingtons lived at F. E. Bernard's ranch home.

Alcorn reported that the Platte Valley's first wedding, officiated by Dr. Huntington, was held March 24, 1889. Nema Ellas and Ralph F. Wilson took their vows on that day.

Along with the Huntingtons and their two eldest daughters, eleven others were listed as communicants in the new church.

Huntington older daughters also became well-known in the small community. Gertrude Huntington became the editor and business manager of the local newspaper, the *Platte Valley Lyre*. She took her position on March 10, 1890. Even in the Territory of Wyoming, which would earn the nickname "the Equality State," women were not yet readily accepted in jobs traditionally considered as men's.

The *Rawlins Daily Times* Centennial Edition reported that Gertrude was "jokingly alluded to as 'Her Editoress.'" As a woman pursuing what was considered a man's career, she was subjected to many comments about "the weaker sex."

Gertrude managed, apparently doing very well. The newspaper also stated that "nothing notably disrespectful about her was published." She supported women's suffrage, and Laura joined her in the newspaper business. Laura served as business manager, beginning her position in October 1890, just a few months after Wyoming earned statehood. Laura worked until several months after her marriage to attorney Alfred S. Heath in 1898. The paper was eventually sold to J.R. Crawford, who consolidated it with the *Saratoga Sun.*

Dr. Huntington lived to see his older daughters work so diligently and successfully in Saratoga. His last official act as a minister was performed at Gertrude's March 28, 1905, wedding to Judge Homer Merrill.

Huntington resigned his Saratoga position in 1903 and returned to Rawlins. He died on May 25, 1905, at the age of eighty-five. Mrs. Huntington lived for more than twenty years after his death. She died August 6, 1925.

Fenimore Chatterton

THE YOUNG MAN WALKED to the White House. A porter let him enter. He was on an important personal mission. He climbed the stairs and entered the President's office.

"I'm Fenimore Chatterton," he said. He explained his goal to become a page for a Supreme Court justice. The teenager felt that such a position would provide a wonderful opportunity to study law.

President Rutherford B. Hayes wrote an introductory note and instructed young Fenimore to take it to the Chief Justice.

Chatterton's spunk would not be rewarded any further in this effort, though it would serve him well in his future endeavors. The Chief Justice had no vacancies available, but he did encourage Chatterton to study law.

And he did. An avid visitor to the Congressional sessions on Saturdays, Chatterton also worked during his teenage years as a "copyist" at a Washington law firm. In spare moments, he accompanied his boss to court, including the Supreme Court. By learning as much as he could about the law and politics, he built a sturdy foundation for his future.

In his youth, he could not have known that the decision of one of the most celebrated murder cases in Wyoming history would fall on his shoulders. As young Chatterton studied law, eventually earning his law degree from the University of Michigan in 1891, he could not have foreseen the cattleman's range wars and the livestock detective that ranchers employed to halt the rampant rustling of their herds. He did not yet know that he would climb to the rank of Governor of Wyoming and decide the fate of a man named Tom Horn.

Fenimore Chatterton was born July 21, 1860, in Oswego, New York. His father, Hammond Chatterton, of German ancestry, became an attorney for the government shortly after the Civil War. The family moved to Washington, D.C., where Chatterton soaked up all the information he could about law.

His mother, Amoret Mazuzan Chatterton, died when her son was only four. "Stepmother difficulties" caused him to live with his mother's sister in Washington, D. C., during the late 1860s.

He enjoyed the outdoors as well as his studious endeavors, rowing and fishing on the Potomac River with friends. If Congress was not in session, Chatterton spent Saturdays at the Smithsonian Institution with naturalists who taught him how to mount animal heads.

His adventures in the West began in 1878, when he came to Wyoming. In *Yesterday's Wyoming*, his memoirs, Chatterton recalled having five dollars in his pocket and a ticket to Chicago when he left Washington in January. In Chicago, he stayed with relatives. The studious young man found a job, but had to walk five miles into the business district and back home each day.

In May, he pawned his watch and traveled to Grinnell, Iowa, where he stayed with an aunt. In Grinnell, Chatterton worked on a farm, milking cows and shocking grain. Later, a job in a grocery store, working twelve hour days, provided him with one dollar per day.

The Teacher's State Institute met in Grinnell to hold exams for new teachers. Chatterton attended, and he earned his certificate. But his destiny was to move even further west.

The post trader at Fort Steele in Wyoming Territory needed a bookkeeper. Chatterton learned of the job from a distant relative, governess for the children of Captain Charles King, stationed at the fort. Salary was fifty dollars each month. Chatterton applied, requesting an additional fifty dollars for traveling expenses.

As often happens to job-seekers, Chatterton received another offer on the heels of this one. Would he be interested in teaching school in the school district of the farmer he'd worked for? Room and board and forty dollars in wages would be paid, and in addition, Chatterton would be expected to do farm chores.

His decision, probably aided by the fifty dollars traveling money sent by J.W. Hugus, the Fort Steele post trader, pushed him west. He arrived at Fort Steele on September 12. This would not be the last time that Chatterton would "gamble on Wyoming's greatness."

He worked as a clerk in the J.W. Hugus General Mercantile and with Hugus's associated banking concern at the fort. He soon learned the business and eventually became the proprietor.

Social life for soldiers at Fort Steele consisted of sailboating or ice skating on the North Platte River, supplemented by an occasional theatrical production by the soldiers. Commissioned officers, along with the post trader and his clerk, affectionately known as "Chat," enjoyed regular dances, luncheons, and card and dinner parties. The men sometimes lunched on a "chicken" salad made by the officers' wives, who used ingredients available to them at the time. The chicken salad was created with jackrabbit meat.

In 1883, Hugus moved to California. He sold the store to Chatterton, who worked in partnership with Wilbur B. Hugus, the post trader's brother, of nearby Warm Springs. Chatterton managed the Fort Steele concern while W. B. Hugus operated "Hugus and Chatterton" in Warm Springs.

Fort Fred Steele was abandoned as a military post in 1886, its services becoming obsolete as the area grew in population and the Indian unrest calmed. Business at Chatterton's store at the fort decreased as customers shopped in Rawlins and Warm Springs, which by now was known as Saratoga.

Chat gave the town its new name in 1884, choosing "Saratoga" because he recalled drinking mineral water at Saratoga Springs, New York, as a five-year-old. The previous name, Warm Springs, had been used because of the popular mineral hot springs located at the site. He also platted the town, beginning in 1885 on the east side of the North Platte River. In 1888, he helped plot the town west of the river.

A larger Hugus and Chatterton store was built on the west side of the river in Saratoga, and soon the merchandise from the Fort Steele store was sent there.

After the military abandoned Fort Steele, Chatterton traveled to Utah to interview for a post trader position there. He wasn't hired, but J.W. Hugus extended another invitation to Chat.

Hugus asked Chat to invest in a new bank and go into the real estate business with him in Four Corners, California. Land prices stood at five hundred dollars per acre, but Chatterton recalled in his memoirs that the land "didn't look any better" than the Fort Steele sagebrush. In the Fort Steele area, land prices stood at $1.25 per acre, boasting the added advantage of plentiful irrigation water.

Chat stuck to his "gamble." He remained in Wyoming.

And there, a political future beckoned to him. In 1888, Chat was elected as the treasurer and probate judge of Carbon County. He soon resigned those positions to seek election as State Senator serving Carbon and Natrona counties. He served in the Wyoming Senate, during the first and second sessions of the State Legislatures in 1890–91 and 1893.

During his first term, Chat served on the committee to create the Great Seal of the State of Wyoming. He proposed eighteen bills during this session, several of which became law. One of the laws, defining the Secretary of State's duties as Acting Governor, held an ominous portent for the legislator. In Wyoming's political framework, the Secretary of State is also the Lieutenant Governor. If something prevents the Governor from performing his duties, the Secretary of State advances to the position of Acting Governor.

Chat had continued studying the law at Fort Steele. He earned admission to the Wyoming Bar in July 1891, and in September entered the University of Michigan's law school, graduating in 1892.

"I returned to Rawlins with one dollar in my pocket, which I gave to a painter to paint a sign—'F. Chatterton, Attorney-at-Law,'" Chatterton recalled in his memoirs.

He located his practice in a small room in the Osborne Building (named for Dr. John Osborne), and soon became partners with David H. Craig, a prosecuting attorney.

In 1891, Chat helped organize the First National Bank of Rawlins with several prominent men of the area, including John C. Davis, Bill Daley, and I.C. Miller.

He continued practicing as an attorney in Rawlins until 1898, when he won election to the office of Secretary of State.

DeForest Richards was elected the Governor of the "Equality State" that same year. The two men campaigned throughout the

Fenimore Chatterton. (Courtesy Carbon County Museum)

state, traveling mostly by buckboard, although portions of the campaign trail were made by riding the railroad.

As a result of their statewide campaign swing, the Republican candidates decided that nearly 1.3 million acres of land in the Big Horn country could be developed for settlement and agricultural purposes through diversion of water from the Big Wind River in Fremont County, and the Big Horn, Greybull, and Shoshone Rivers in Big Horn County.

Chatterton stated in his memoirs that their plan resulted in the construction of several Wyoming towns, including Riverton, Shoshoni, Worland, Lovell, and Powell.

"Governor DeForest Richards' administration accomplished more for the agricultural settlement and for the livestock interests of Wyoming than any other administration up to date," Chatterton wrote in his memoirs published in 1957. He attributed the achievements to the fifteen hundred mile buckboard ride the men took as candidates.

In 1902, Richards and Chatterton won re-election as Governor and Secretary of State. Chatterton's earlier work in the legislature soon affected his future. Richards died on April 28, 1903, following surgery. Chatterton ascended to the Governor's seat, as provided by Wyoming law.

The position was a challenging one, and Chatterton faced an especially difficult decision in 1903. Tom Horn, the range detective, had been convicted in 1902 of murdering fourteen-year-old Willie Nickell the year before. The case gained national attention, and the eyes of the nation rested on Fenimore Chatterton. Would the Governor pardon Tom Horn?

Horn was sentenced to hang on January 9, 1903. His attorneys appealed the decision, taking the case to the Wyoming Supreme Court, which sustained the lower court's position. The Supreme Court set November 20, 1903, as the new date for Horn's execution.

Members of the cattle industry were suspected of hiring Horn to eliminate cattle rustlers, sheep producers, and homesteaders who encroached on lands claimed by large cattlemen as their grazing ranges. Horn was also suspected of killing Matt Rash and Isom Dart in 1900, although he was never charged.

The range detective had confessed to the Nickell murder to Joe LeFors, Deputy United States Marshal, who pretended to hire him to do a job in Montana. As LeFors loosened Horn's tongue with liquor and encouraged him to brag about his exploits, a stenographer and deputy sheriff listened to the conversation from the next room. Horn was arrested, charged, tried, and given the death penalty.

On November 1, 1903, Horn's attorneys applied to Governor Chatterton for a commutation of the death sentence, asking that it be reduced to life imprisonment.

Chatterton received death threats and threats against his political career if he refused to commute Horn's sentence. With pressure building, Chatterton double-checked the facts presented at the trial. He cross-examined witnesses brought forward after the trial.

Time ticked away for Tom Horn, waiting in jail.

The Governor decided. Though he stated in his decision that he personally opposed capital punishment, Chatterton wrote that he must abide by the laws of Wyoming.

He wrote, "I do not believe, in the absence of extenuating circumstances, and there are none in this case, the commutation, reprieve or pardon power was given to the Governor for the purpose of enabling him to reverse the judgments of the courts, unless, in his best judgment from competent evidence adduced—by competent evidence, I mean such as could be introduced on behalf of the defendant in trial court—he believes the wrong, otherwise irreparable, has been committed."

As soon as Governor Chatterton signed this decision, on November 14, 1903, Tom Horn's fate became a noose around his neck.

Cheyenne, the capital city, anticipated the hanging with people placing bets on whether the event would actually occur or not. Governor Chatterton received information that a rescue attempt was being planned for the convicted man. He called in troops to guard the prisoner and the courthouse and jail until after the execution.

Tom Horn was hung. Controversy lingers around the case, however. In 1995, the Tom Horn trial was re-created. Jurors in this trial acquitted the range detective. Members of the Nickell family, feeling that people should not meddle with history, did not approve of the re-trial.

Fenimore Chatterton might not have approved either. However, the decision he rendered determined his own fate. His term as Governor ended in 1905.

In 1906, Chatterton retired from political life and moved to Riverton, where he practiced law. He became an instrumental force in the building of a branch of the Northwestern Railroad through to Lander.

However, he didn't lose his interest in Carbon County. He took an active role in the building of the Saratoga and Encampment Railroad, which was to serve the booming copper industry in the Encampment area.

In 1905, Chatterton became president of the Saratoga and Encampment Railroad Company, which had paid the debt of the Yellowstone Pacific Railway Company. The Yellowstone planned to run a rail route through the Saratoga area from Denver to Yellowstone Park. Chatterton, however, wanted the train route to extend from Encampment to Walcott, Wyoming. The renowned Ferris-Haggarty mine, located near Encampment, produced a good portion of Wyoming's copper at the time.

The first train appeared in Saratoga on July 18, 1907, six years after completion of the line. Residents of the town held a large fish fry to commemorate the train's arrival. By August 1908, tracks had been laid to Encampment.

The railroad might have succeeded, but bad timing precluded it from becoming a financial success. The Encampment copper mining days came to an abrupt close in 1908. Two fires at the smelter created enough hardship, but in that same year, the copper mining industry collapsed.

The railroad, which hauled passengers, lumber products, and livestock at a snail's pace and earned the nickname "Slow and Easy," operated throughout several bouts of financial difficulties until the late 1960s. Tracks for the old line remain between Saratoga and Walcott, used now only to haul lumber from the Louisiana-Pacific lumber mill.

Chatterton continued to practice law in Riverton, where he raised livestock and farmed in addition to pursuing his railroad ventures, until 1927. In that year, he became a member of the Public Service Commission and the State Board of Equalization, spending more time in state governmental service.

🐚🐚🐚

Chatterton had married Stella Wyland on September 12, 1900, and the couple had two daughters, Eleanor and Constance. He wrote in his memoirs that his family helped him, especially with the Riverton Town and Irrigation project. He credited "much of the successes and happiness of my life" to his wife.

In 1936, he retired, moving to Arvada, Colorado. He was active in the Masonic Lodge, receiving the Thirty-third Degree, the highest honor of work awarded. He maintained his affiliation with a

Wyoming lodge, and at the time of his death, he was the oldest living Grand Master of Wyoming.

The spunky young chap who had walked right into President Rutherford B. Hayes's office secured his place in Wyoming's history through his political and legal acumen and his contributions to the state's business community. He died in 1958 in Shreveport, Louisiana, at the age of ninety-seven.

The stone remains of some of the buildings that made up Wyoming's first coal town, Carbon, still stand at the site amidst sagebrush and rattlesnakes. The town only existed for about thirty years, from 1868 to 1902. Seven coal mines fed the Union Pacific locomotives traveling along the recently completed transcontinental railroad.

In its heyday, its population reached 1,200 and included professionals such as a doctor, lawyer, dentist and photographer. Carbon also had the first state-chartered bank in Wyoming, the Carbon State Bank.

As the wind whispers secrets among the sagebrush, Carbon's past provides many interesting tales of Wyoming's history, complete with outlaws and hangings.

The railroad soon traveled to nearby Hanna, where coal reserves were larger. Relegated to a spur rather than the main line, Carbon soon faded away.

The cemetery, just over the hill from the townsite, contains the grave of Sheriff's Deputy Robert Widdowfield, a marble monument forever testifying to his murder at the hands of Big Nose George.

Sources of information: *Annals of Wyoming*, Vol. 19, No. 1, January, 1947;
Ghost Towns of Wyoming, by Mary Lou Pence and Lola Homsher;
Richard Fisher's presentation to the
Saratoga Historical & Cultural Association's 1995 trek to Carbon

Big Nose George

Big Nose George Parrott—a man so infamous, so notorious, that not only was he lynched for his crime of murdering a deputy, but his skin was made into shoes worn by a governor and his skullcap became a doorstop for the state's first woman doctor.

This violent death and the bizarre treatment of his corpse has made the outlaw both the center of colorful legends and a prime candidate for scientific research.

His life remains a mystery which may soon be unraveled through a university study on frontier violence, using scientific and technological methods which have only recently become available.

But what kind of life led to this gruesome fate?

The bandit, whose real name was apparently George Francis Warden, had held a legitimate job as a bull team driver over the Cheyenne-Black Hills freight route before he turned to crime. Soon, however, he was robbing travelers on the Oregon Trail along the Sweetwater River. Eventually he progressed from stagecoach robberies to train robberies.

Confusion exists even over his name. Some sources indicate the bandit's name was Joe Maneuse, but many researchers believe Maneuse was another man arrested at about the same time. Big Nose George gave his name as George Francis Warden at the time of his final arrest. He was also know as George Parrott, the surname thought by some to be a reference to his beak-like nose and by others to be derivative of the French name Parrotte. But most often, he was known as Big Nose George.

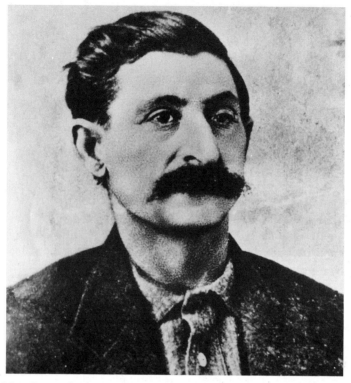

Big Nose George aka George Parrott. (Courtesy Carbon County Museum)

George Parrott had a poor reputation before he entered Carbon County. He had earlier been arrested for horse theft and had been tried before a Justice of the Peace. But he had an alibi and was acquitted. Even so, his reputation as a crook endured.

According to Charles Kelly in *The Outlaw Trail,* Parrott had also headquartered at one time behind the red wall in Hole-in-the-Wall country near Kaycee, Wyoming, along with other outlaws of the time, including Jesse and Frank James, Persimmon Bill, Teton Jackson, Dutch Henry, and Black Hank.

The final and oft-told tale of George's outlaw career revolves around a failed train robbery attempt in 1878. Big Nose George and his gang schemed to rob the payroll train as it came to the coal town of Carbon, so they removed spikes from a rail near Medicine Bow to delay the train. Included in this gang was a man known as Dutch Charley Burris, who would also become a guest of honor at a necktie party.

A railroad employee, checking the track, grew wise to this scheme and calmly notified the train station at Como to delay the train. A posse, led by two sheriff's deputies, Robert Widdowfield and "Tip" Vincent, trailed the bandits. The outlaws fled to the west side of Elk Mountain near the head of Rattlesnake Creek.

The deputies followed the trail and tracked the bandits to a recently abandoned campfire on the creek. As they examined the still warm embers, they were shot and killed there. The murders occurred on August 19, 1878.

Widdowfield's friends and his wife, Ann, spent many hours waiting for the thirty-three-year-old deputy to return with the outlaw in tow on that hot August day.

When he didn't, they searched the area. Finding the bodies of Widdowfield and Vincent hidden in the brush and stripped of valuables, the deputies' friends vowed they'd "right the wrong." The Union Pacific and Carbon County offered a reward of one thousand dollars each for the villains.

The story of the capture of Dutch Charley is recorded in the *History of the Union Pacific Coal Mines*. The LeFevre brothers captured the bandit and took him to Laramie's jail. Sheriff James Rankin, brother of the heroic rider, Joe Rankin, escorted him back to Rawlins, the county seat. A stop for coal and water at Carbon on January 23, 1879, proved hazardous to the outlaw, however.

Men in the town of Carbon were waiting for their chance at revenge. They took charge of the locomotive when the train stopped. Dutch Charley was hauled off the train. They took him to the Beckwith-Quinn store. According to the Union Pacific history, the bandit pleaded for forgiveness as he was escorted down the dusty street.

"Don't string me up!" he pleaded, begging to be shot instead. The residents of the town were enraged by the death of their deputy friends. They felt that Dutch Charley should not meet any better fate. Their friends hadn't earned a sporting chance, they reasoned. Why should this criminal?

Despite his pleas, Dutch Charley was strung up from a telegraph pole, and a man kicked the barrel from beneath him.

In the book, *Ghost Towns of Wyoming*, Mary Lou Pence and Lola Homsher wrote that Dutch Charley confessed to the crimes just before he was hung. He also said, "Joe Maneuse, he...." Then Frank Howard kicked the barrel from beneath his feet.

Howard was "one of his pals in crime" who had turned state's witness. He apparently was afraid of what Charley might tell if he was allowed to finish his sentence, so he gladly hastened his departure. Pence and Homsher reported that Howard "immediately left town, grabbing a freight train about a mile east."

In a varying account, a *Rawlins Daily Times* article in November 1995 reported that Widdowfield's sister-in-law kicked the barrel from beneath Dutch Charley. Whoever it was, Dutch Charley was considered unworthy of burial in the Carbon Cemetery. His unmarked grave is located somewhere outside of the cemetery's boundaries, amidst the abundant sagebrush. A marble monument in the cemetery still stands as a memorial to Widdowfield.

Meanwhile, Big Nose George was still on the loose. He escaped to Montana, but even he would not elude capture for much longer. In July 1880, he was caught in Miles City. His arraignment took place in Rawlins on September 13, 1880.

Indecision reigned through his court actions. First, the bandit pled guilty at his arraignment. Then, just four days later, he changed his plea to not guilty. In November, his attorney filed for a change of venue because of prejudice by Jacob B. Blair, the presiding judge. The Honorable William W. Peck, associate justice of the Supreme Court, was called to preside over the case.

The jury was sworn in on November 16, 1880. They heard testimony the next day. On November 18, Big Nose George again changed his plea. He pled guilty. A motion was filed for arrest of judgment and sentence. The court took the matter under advisement, but denied the motion on December 15. Big Nose George was sentenced to hang; the event was scheduled for April 2, 1881. He remained imprisoned in the Carbon County jail in Rawlins.

Citizens of the area—furious at the heinous crime the outlaw had committed—weren't going to wait that long to see that justice was served. Osborne recalled in a signed statement given to the Union Pacific Historical Museum in Omaha that the lynch mob asked him to be present "for the purpose of telling them when the prisoner was dead, as they did not want to run the slightest risk."

A week before the scheduled hanging of Big Nose, the outlaw overpowered jailor Bob Rankin at dinner. (Some accounts mistakenly report Rankin as the sheriff. Mark Miller, great-grandson of Sheriff I. C. Miller, believes his great-grandfather was probably collecting taxes on Sand Creek at the time of the incident.) Osborne recalled that Big Nose George had somehow gotten a "case knife," and he sawed through the rivets on his heavy homemade leg shackles. He struck Rankin with the shackles and tried to make a run for it. Rosa Rankin, the jailor's wife, discovered the bandit's attempted escape.

According to *History of the Union Pacific Coal Mines*, she "slammed the cell door and ran to the jail steps where she fired her husband's revolver into the air." At her signal, numerous men ran to the jail, grabbed Big Nose George, and took the prisoner outside.

According to Osborne, they tied his hands behind his back and placed him on an empty kerosene barrel, noose around his neck. They kicked the barrel out from beneath him. But Big Nose George, infamous bandit and killer, would not die so easily.

The rope broke.

He fell and begged to be shot. The angry citizens did not comply with this request. Instead, they got a twelve-foot ladder and made him climb it, again placing a noose on his neck. He had worked his hands free from the ropes that held him and now grasped the ladder. They pulled the ladder away. The heavy weight of the repaired leg-irons pulled him down as he struggled to hold onto a nearby pole. Osborne said the bandit choked to death. Osborne gave the leg-irons, made and repaired by Rawlins blacksmith James Candlish, to J.C. Gale, who gave them to the Union Pacific Historical Museum, along with the doctor's signed 1928 statement. (Candlish is also credited with creating the sheepwagon.)

The lynching took place on March 22, 1881. The jail register of the day, displayed now at the Carbon County Museum in Rawlins, declared the murderer "went to jine the angels" that day.

An inquest concluded that Big Nose George met his death by hanging at the hands of unknown persons.

As part of the postmortem examination following Parrott's death, portions of his skin were removed by Dr. John Osborne. These were tanned and made into the shoes worn by Osborne at his gubernatorial inauguration (*see* chapter on Osborne). The top of Parrott's skull was sawed in half, and his brain was examined for abnormalities; the skullcap came into the possession of young Dr. Lillian Heath, Osborne's assistant (*see* section on Lillian Heath Nelson). Dr. Osborne also made a plaster of paris death mask of Big Nose George. Then Parrott's body was placed in a whiskey barrel and buried.

But that was not the end of Big Nose George.

During the 1950s workmen discovered a barrel buried in a Rawlins alley. It was exhumed and found to contain a skeleton, missing the skullcap. Dr. Heath, then well into her eighties, identified the bones by matching the skullcap, which she'd been using as a doorstop, with the other portion of the skull. It was a perfect fit. The body, with the exception of the lower portion of the skull which was donated to Carbon County Museum, was reburied.

❀❀❀

The postmortem, macabre as it was, insured that physical evidence used for modern-day scientific study was available—skin, bones, fragments of flesh.

Forensic scientists at University of Wyoming (UW) in Laramie have been working for several years on a project examining the remains of seventy-eight white people on the frontier. The Big Nose George study is part of the project being conducted by Kristi McMahan, a graduate student at UW. Through the scientific miracle of DNA testing, scientists hope to learn more about the outlaw's life. McMahan is working with Dr. George Gill, UW anthropology professor and forensic science-osteology specialist, and Dr. Mark Miller, also a UW anthropology instructor and Wyoming's state archeologist. (This is the same Mark Miller who is Sheriff I.C. Miller's great-grandson.)

McMahan stated that Parrott's story, with the "oral traditions and historical records to compare and contrast with osteological data" make the outlaw an excellent research specimen.

As part of McMahan's 1996 master's thesis focusing on violence on the frontier, the two portions of Big Nose George's skull were reunited for the first time in forty-five years. The skullcap, donated to the Union Pacific Historical Museum in Omaha, Nebraska, by

Dr. Lillian Heath, and the lower portion of the skull, from the Carbon County Museum collection, were photographed and measured.

The large nose that Parrott is famous for possibly indicates that he is of French Mediterranean descent, according to Gill. The scientists hope to discover from which of two families he is descended.

The scientific evidence may support local tales. Gill, quoted in a 1995 *Rawlins Times* article, stated, "I've found that the folklore of violent episodes in the West is sometimes more accurate than the documented history."

In addition, the only known photograph of Big Nose George, taken in Omaha, Nebraska, after his capture, is being tested for authenticity by Dr. Michael Charney of Colorado State University in Fort Collins, Colorado. Photos of the rearticulated skullcap and face will be superimposed over the photograph to prove the outlaw's identity.

The UW study has proven, to Dr. Gill's satisfaction, that the skullcap matches the lower part. When the pieces were reunited, scientists made a "good, accurate cast" which will be reproduced for museums, Gill said.

The DNA test was taken from a piece of flesh still attached to the upper part of the skull, Gill said. Though results are not yet in, Gill said that a crime lab representative stated that his examination of the follicle pattern leaves no doubt that the skin of the shoes is, in fact, human skin. The testing of the shoes will probably end with that, since examiners do not want to destroy the shoes to obtain a DNA sample large enough to conclusively state that the skin is really that of Big Nose George.

Gill said that the analysis so far has proven that people have not been exaggerating about the gruesome tale of the outlaw. "It looks solid to us," Gill said. Kristi McMahan will return to UW to continue her research on the project.

So this is not the end of Big Nose George.

❦

"Rawlins has had a hard name all through the country, owing to the frequency of such shooting scrapes in an early day, but of late years there has been less affrays and disturbances here than in any town in the Territory, and it was fast becoming impressed upon all that the bad name was totally undeserved, and that the inhabitants of our town were peaceful, law-abiding citizens. Lately, however, we have had quite a series of shooting scrapes and some color is thereby given to the old reputation."

From an article in the *Carbon County Journal,* November 15, 1879, which reported a shooting incident and the findings of the jury selected to investigate. Sheriff James G. Rankin of Carbon County and Private Anthony Hobert of Company M Third Cavalry shot a "mule skinner on the rampage" and were fully exonerated by the jury.

John E. Osborne

THE PHRASE "WALK A MILE in another man's shoes" usually means that a person should try to imagine himself in another's place or empathize with someone coping with difficult times. The phrase takes on a gruesome aspect when applied to a certain pair of shoes worn by Dr. John E. Osborne.

While serving as a physician in Rawlins, Dr. Osborne was present during the hanging of the outlaw Big Nose George. No family claimed the notorious bandit's body, so Dr. Thomas Maghee used it for medical study. Dr. Osborne skinned the torso and had a pair of two-tone shoes and a medical bag made from the tanned skin.

Local residents recall that the doctor made a braided buggy whip with other parts of the skin, which he presented to the nephew of Deputy Robert Widdowfield. Big Nose George had murdered Deputy Widdowfield as the deputy tracked him in connection with an attempted train robbery.

The shoes were displayed for some time in a glass case in the lobby of the Rawlins National Bank when Dr. Osborne served as chairman of the board of the financial institution. E.W. Walck, Sr., remembers going into the bank as a child with his father in the 1930s. Osborne let him touch the shoes as he told the tale of Big Nose George's lynching. Walck also recalls the doctor explaining that he paid the undertaker five dollars not to bury Big Nose George's body too deeply, so they could easily disinter it.

The shoes are now displayed in a glass case in the Carbon County Museum in Rawlins. Joyce Kelley, curator at the museum, said Osborne wore the shoes "considerably," as well as at his inauguration as Governor of Wyoming. "He was very proud of his project," she said.

Not all facets of Osborne's life were so grim. Like Fenimore Chatterton, John E. Osborne was born in New York state. He, like Chatterton after him, would climb the political ladder to earn the position of Governor of Wyoming. His aspirations took him even higher than state politics. Osborne became congressman from Wyoming and later served as First Assistant Secretary of State during the administration of President Woodrow Wilson.

Although he may be best remembered for his political strengths and foibles, Osborne's first chosen career was medicine.

🐝🌽🐝

John E. Osborne was born in Westport, Essex County, New York, on June 19, 1858. As a teenager, Osborne apprenticed with a Vermont druggist. He graduated from the University of Vermont in 1880, earning his degree in medicine and surgery.

The West beckoned. He traveled to Rawlins in 1881, becoming the appointed surgeon for the Union Pacific Railroad there, a position he held until 1887.

In 1884, Dr. Osborne purchased the Rawlins Drug, a company founded in 1876. The wood structure stood next door to the Rankin Brothers Livery and Stables. That building was later moved to what is now the Rawlins National Bank parking lot.

In 1901, the drugstore moved into a sandstone building which Osborne had built using locally quarried red stone. Dr. Osborne would not begin construction of the building until the city provided sewer service. Dr. Osborne's office and apartments were located on the second floor of the new stone structure. The structure, now known as the Osborne Building, still stands at the corner of Fifth and Cedar Streets in Rawlins.

In 1884, soon after his arrival in Rawlins, Osborne entered the livestock industry. He would become known as one of the largest individual sheep owners in Wyoming Territory. Within the next decade, Wyoming's livestock industry would become caught up in a whirlwind of controversial events. And so would Osborne.

During the next few years, Osborne entered the political arena. The years 1887–88 proved to be busy for the doctor, years in which he worked in a couple of political capacities. Osborne won election as the second mayor of Rawlins. He also served as the Chairman of

Dr. John E. Osborne. (Courtesy Carbon County Museum)

the Territorial Penitentiary Commission. (The Territorial Legislature had awarded the principal towns of each of the original five Wyoming counties with one state institution each. The penitentiary was assigned to Rawlins.)

The building still stands on Walnut Street in Rawlins, now known as Wyoming's Frontier Prison, with guided tours provided for interested parties. The building originally stood north of the present town, which has now grown enough to include it within the city limits. A new penitentiary was constructed in 1981 and is located on the south side of town.

In 1892, Osborne was elected as an alternate to the Democratic National Convention. That same year, Osborne defeated Republican Edward Ivinson, a Laramie banker, in the gubernatorial race.

The bitter campaign stirred resentments, as several heated issues faced Wyoming voters, and the concept of "fusion" came to the forefront. The Populist party held its first national nominating convention but emerged in state politics as only a minor force.

According to T.A. Larson in *History of Wyoming*, the Populists accepted the Democrats' proposal for "fusion" and agreed to support Osborne, running along with H.A. Coffeen of Sheridan as the Democratic Congressional candidate, in exchange for support for James B. Weaver, the Populist candidate for President.

Republicans and Populists "fused" in the southern part of the state while Democrats and Populists merged their northern efforts. The Democrats, with enthusiastic agreement from the Populists, used the Johnson County War, the infamous invasion of cattlemen fighting to protect the open range, to increase resentment against the Republicans.

The issue produced such deep rifts that some Democrats were expelled from the party because they defended the Wyoming Stock Growers Association. Though the Johnson County War served as the major issue during the 1892 campaign, free coinage of silver also emerged as a divisive problem. Senator F. E. Warren's Arid Lands Bill of 1891created controversy, too.

Larson wrote that partisan critics of Dr. Osborne considered him "an agnostic, a dude" who was stubborn and lacked humor. These critics also stated that the doctor left "his finger marks on every five cent piece that passes through his hands."

Both gubernatorial candidates received similar treatment by partisan presses who criticized them as wealthy men with few other political qualities.

Dr. Osborne emerged as the victor. He carried all the Wyoming counties except Laramie, earning 9,290 votes to Ivinson's 7,509. In addition, Henry A. Coffeen earned election to Congress. But the unpleasantness shown in the campaign did not end with the election.

Larson stated that once Osborne was elected to the Governor's post, he had "a comic-opera time of it."

Controversy surrounded the governor's office. Newspapers reported the returns showing that Osborne had won. At the time, the elected person was to assume the duties and powers of governor when elected. But Osborne, though assured of his victory, had not received official confirmation from Cheyenne.

He traveled to the capital city on December 2 and arranged for a notary public to give him the oath of office. He took the position of governor, issuing a proclamation stating that he was "duly and legally qualified" to take office.

Acting Governor Amos Barber claimed that Osborne's action was "usurpation," and stated that the delay in official returns was caused because returns from Fremont and Converse counties had not yet been received.

Osborne issued another proclamation, stating that the delay was due to a conspiracy to change election results for certain members of the legislature and to ensure the election of a certain candidate for U.S. Senate.

On December 8, the canvassing board met and declared Osborne the winner. Governor Osborne officially assumed his duties on January 2, 1893. The Wyoming Supreme Court later called his assumption of duties in December as "premature and invalid."

Osborne requested that legislators revise the election laws to prevent future problems when he addressed the Second State Legislature. The election laws were not amended until 1897. The laws provided for a canvass of the vote within thirty days of the election, with a certificate presented by the governor to each officially elected candidate.

Osborne said, "The gaze of the nation has, for weeks past, been fixed upon Wyoming, in view of the attempted bold fraud of unscrupulous political bosses to reverse the will of the voters, as emphatically expressed at the ballot box."

Larson stated that the legislature spent more time on "intrigues and joint sessions" than it did on actual lawmaking. Only thirty-three laws were adopted, with six resolutions and memorials.

The new governor urged legislators to reduce the powers and regulations that had been entrusted to the Board of Livestock Commissioners, seeking to abrogate the commission, but no action was taken on the issue.

Osborne exercised another power to make his feelings clear. He vetoed an appropriation of funds for the livestock board. The Wyoming Stock Growers Association then had to supply the board with funds for the next two years. He also vetoed a request from the board's secretary requesting reimbursement of funds used to pay a clerk.

The free coinage issue came to the front as well. Silver was maintained on a proportional parity with gold at the time, and although Wyoming was not a large silver producer, it had an interest in doing so along with other western states which produced the metal. Osborne recommended that Wyoming elect a senator who would help Wyoming achieve a position as one of the states advocating "free and unlimited coinage" of silver.

The Legislature adopted a memorial to Congress in favor of free and unlimited silver coinage at the ration that existed prior to the Demonetization Act of 1873. The memorial, approved by Osborne and signed by the Speaker of the House, carried another recognizable Wyoming signature as well, that of Fenimore Chatterton, Vice President of the Senate.

Osborne recommended completion of the penitentiary building at Rawlins. The original appropriations for funding the work on the building had been made in 1888. Construction on the structure had ended after more than $31,000 had been expended. Not enough work on the original building had been completed to protect it from the weather and elements. The Legislature's act of 1893 levied a three-quarters of a mil tax for that year and a one-half mil for 1894 to fund completion of the penitentiary.

During the legislative session, turmoil resulted around the ballot for a U.S. Senate seat. At the time, U.S. Senators were selected by the state legislature. After thirty ballots, no senator had been selected. The twenty-three Republicans, twenty-one Democrats, and five Populists could not agree, and no ballot received the twenty-five votes necessary for approval. Allegations of bribery and the possible poisoning of a legislator contributed to the suspense and confusion.

The legislators did approve a memorial to Congress favoring popular election of United States senators. Governor Osborne appointed A.C. Beckwith of Evanston to fill the vacant seat, but controversy surrounded even this decision.

Francis E. Warren had hoped to be appointed to the position by Amos Barber, who would have served as Acting Governor if Osborne had left the state to attend the inauguration of President Cleveland. But Osborne did not travel to Washington.

Meanwhile, Beckwith waited for months to be officially seated, and he resigned in August. After a similar circumstance in Montana, the U.S. Senate decided that the state legislature should meet in special session to choose a replacement. Osborne did not call a special session to choose a new senator, and Wyoming was represented by only one senator from 1893–95, relying solely on Senator Joseph M. Carey.

Osborne declined the nomination for Governor in 1896, but served as a delegate to the Democratic National Convention.

Silver again played a role in the 1896 campaign. Osborne still supported free coinage of the precious metal. He ran for Wyoming's seat in the House of Representatives, defeating Republican Frank W. Mondell in a close election.

In 1898, he ran for the United States Senate but was defeated in the general election. He continued his work in politics, serving as a member of the Democratic National Committee from 1900 to 1920.

In 1907, Dr. Osborne married Selina Smith of Princeton, Kentucky. The couple had one daughter, Jean Curtis, who was born the next year.

In 1913, Osborne began a two-year position as the First Assistant United States Secretary of State. In the Wyoming election of 1918, Osborne again ran for the U.S. Senate but was defeated by Warren. According to Larson, Republicans portrayed the former governor as a carpetbagger because he had lived in Denver for awhile, and they used the 1892 election squabbles against him as well.

Some people took a dim view of the doctor issuing prescriptions which were filled at his Rawlins drugstore, feeling that he made a fortune by playing both sides of the medical field—both prescribing and selling drugs. Despite all the political hullabaloo, Osborne was a popular candidate.

In 1926, Dr. Osborne and his family traveled the globe on the Cunard cruise ship "Laconia." Highlights of the trip were written by Dr. T.J. Swisher of Rawlins and published in two installments in 1926 issues of the *Rawlins Republican*.

In 1928, the newspaper carried a report on Dr. Osborne's presentation on Egypt to Rawlins High School students. The students enjoyed the program so much that they asked Osborne to give more programs.

The paper reported that Osborne took students from the pyramids to the city of Alexandria with his "fascinating" talk. He showed the students a fossilized foot of one of the ancient Egyptians which had been recovered from a buried desert city near Cairo.

Dr. Osborne died April 24, 1943, in Rawlins. He was buried at Princeton, Kentucky, where his wife was interred.

Butch Cassidy

IN NOVEMBER 1902, the *Cheyenne Daily Leader* reported that Butch Cassidy had been in the Grand Encampment district after an absence of more than three years. The report states, "... the officers here did not even know of his presence until he had taken his departure as quickly and mysteriously as he dropped into town."

Mystery continues to surround the outlaw born George (some sources say Robert) LeRoy Parker, but known throughout the world as Butch Cassidy, he paid visits to Carbon County spanning several years.

His sister, Lula Parker Betenson, quoted in the *Wyoming Eagle* in 1974, called Cassidy "a good boy who got off on the wrong foot."

Cassidy and his bunch of outlaws, the Wild Bunch, also frequently stopped in Baggs and the Little Snake River valley area. Jane Sielaff, the director of the Little Snake River Museum in Savery, Wyoming, said that Cassidy and the Wild Bunch once sought the services of the local doctor, Dr. Noyes.

According to Sielaff, the outlaws got along well with people in the area. There were only a few misunderstandings, she said, but when the bandits stayed in the area they worked as ranch hands on different ranches and were considered good workers. Several young ladies "from prominent families" in the region married members of the Wild Bunch, the museum director said.

An article written by Kathryn Wright, published in *True West* in 1979, said Boyd Charter's aunt married into the Wild Bunch. Charter, the son of Bert Charter, who rode with the bunch, said that people working on the film, *Butch Cassidy and the Sundance Kid*, approached his aunt hoping she'd tell the whole story. Even though his aunt could have profited from explaining what happened, she didn't. His aunt told Boyd Charter that she had vowed never to talk about the Wild Bunch—and she didn't.

The Sundance Kid, Harry Longabaugh, long-time sidekick of Cassidy's, traded a gun to a Little Snake River area rancher for supplies. The rifle is displayed at the museum. "Sundance" earned his nickname after serving time in the Sundance, Wyoming, jail for horse theft.

🦋🦋

Perhaps Butch Cassidy's most famous Wyoming deed was the Tipton train robbery, which took place on August 29, 1900. A 1977 article in the *Rawlins Daily Times* called the robbery "one of the events which marked the beginning of the end of the Wild Bunch and the end of an era."

The bandits blew up the safe in the express car of the second section of westbound Union Pacific Number Three, hoping for a good amount of cash. Newspaper accounts stated that the group netted around one hundred dollars for their troubles. An estimated two thousand dollars in damage was done to the express car.

The robbery occurred about two-and-a-half miles from Tipton, about fifty-five miles west of Rawlins. It was thought that Cassidy had inside information about a shipment of government money to be sent to the Philippines. The outlaw apparently hoped to strike it rich and leave the country.

By the time the Tipton robbery took place, Cassidy had been involved in the crime business for more than a decade. Called the "Robin Hood of the West," the outlaw served some time in the Wyoming penitentiary in 1894 when he was twenty-seven years old.

Cassidy served one-and-one-half years of his prison term in Laramie. He was pardoned by the governor, William A. Richards, on January 19, 1896, on the condition that he stay out of Wyoming. Cassidy, though he was arrested four times during his life, was never imprisoned again.

Controversy still surrounds Butch Cassidy. Some accounts state that Cassidy and Harry Longabaugh were killed in 1908 in San Vicente, Bolivia. But doubts persist.

Lula Betenson, Cassidy's sister, stated in the 1974 *Wyoming Eagle* report that her brother did not die in Bolivia. She did not say what really happened, however, leaving the issue open for speculation.

In the same article, Betenson's claim was disputed by William C. Linn, the president of the Pinkerton Detective Agency. Linn said that the Pinkerton file on Cassidy contained sworn statements of witnesses who saw the bodies of Cassidy and Longabaugh, who were shot by the Bolivian army. Linn stated that no solid evidence supported the theory that Cassidy and Longabaugh returned to the United States.

A 1990 *Casper Star-Tribune* article, published a decade after Betenson's death, reported she had claimed that Cassidy returned to America and lived, using an assumed name, until at least 1937 as a businessman.

That claim perhaps lends some credibility to the theory promoted by Larry Pointer in his book, *In Search of Butch Cassidy*. Pointer stated that Cassidy, using the name William T. Phillips, had lived in Spokane, Washington. Though he designed many mechanical devices, they did not make money for the former outlaw, who also suffered business failures throughout the Depression era.

Pointer stated that Cassidy returned to Wyoming in 1936 to search for valuables that the Wild Bunch had stored in the Wind River Mountains, but he didn't find the treasures. According to Pointer, Cassidy died on July 30, 1937, of old age.

In 1991, PBS television's science program, NOVA, sponsored the exhumation of the grave in the San Vicente (Bolivia) cemetery thought to contain Butch Cassidy. Forensic scientists performed DNA tests on the Caucasian skeleton they found. The DNA results showed the skeleton was not Butch nor Sundance. Later research proved the grave was that of Gustav Zimmer, a German.

Whatever became of Butch Cassidy, much information has been written about his escapades. In *The Outlaw Trail*, Charles Kelly stated that Cassidy "never lacked courage to take a chance," but the outlaw never killed a man until his last stand in South America. Kelly attributed Cassidy's success in avoiding lawmen to his "ability to keep cool in an emergency" and his temperate use of liquor.

🌿🌿🌿

Butch Cassidy. (Courtesy Wyoming Division of Cultural Resources)

Butch Cassidy, born George LeRoy Parker in 1866, was the oldest child of Maximilian and Ann Campbell Parker's brood of seven. The Parkers purchased a ranch near Circleville, Utah, which would influence their son's career.

A ranch hand who had worked for the previous owners decided to stay on to help the Parkers. Mike Cassidy had been an active member of a group of horse thieves and cattle rustlers, and he soon became a mentor to young George.

Mike taught him to ride, rope, shoot, and brand. When Mike's herd of cattle, acquired during his employment on the ranch, grew so large that it began attracting suspicion, he moved it. George helped, herding the cattle into an area which would later become known as Robber's Roost.

Mike traveled to Mexico to avoid facing difficulties with the law, and George took his last name. He was known as George Cassidy for awhile, later using the nickname Butch. Some sources say he got the nickname after working in a Rock Springs butcher shop, taking the name Cassidy so his exploits would not dishonor the Parkers.

Kelly wrote that during one of Cassidy's first horse thefts the outlaw rode away after taking horses from officers who had trailed him. Realizing that he had their canteens, he returned to the site and gave the canteens back. Kelly called the incident a "good illustration of [Cassidy's] methods in later years and in tighter places."

By 1892, Cassidy and a partner, Al Hainer, had become horse traders in the Wind River country of Wyoming. Unsuspecting neighbors didn't realize that the "traders" always sold, but never bought, horses. The partners sold out in the spring of 1893 because it had been a particularly severe winter. Thousands of head of livestock had frozen to death, and people in the area had been plagued with the flu. Cassidy headquartered in Lander.

The Wild Bunch was sometimes known as the Powder Springs gang, because Cassidy had built a cabin on Powder Springs. Their meeting place was the tiny Wyoming town of Baggs. The bandits often tore up the town when they visited, but they always paid for the damages when they left. Cassidy earned a reputation as a "skilled harmonicist" who entertained the bunch during their parties.

Wright quoted Boyd Charter, "'The Bunch would ride to Baggs, get drunk and shoot things up,' Boyd says. 'One time, my dad told me, they shot the heads off twelve chickens. They took them into the hotel, gave my mother Maud a $5 gold piece for each one and told her to cook them for supper.'"

The name "Wild Bunch" came when the U. S. declared war on Spain, according to Kelly. The outlaws around Brown's Hole, patriotic as they were, decided to meet in Steamboat Springs, Colorado, to form a troop of cavalry which would be called "the Wild Bunch."

However, the outlaws feared what their status would be if they joined the army. Deciding that they might be arrested if they enlisted in the service, they didn't participate in the war effort. The name stuck, though.

Kelly's account gives credit for Cassidy's arrest in Wyoming for horse theft to Bob Calverly, although other sources name Uinta County Sheriff John Ward as the arresting officer. Calverly was a Texan who served as chief deputy for Governor William A. Richards and also had been a lieutenant in Theodore Roosevelt's Rough Riders.

With the assistance of a Montana sheriff, Calverly tussled with the outlaw. Cassidy used the Montana man as a shield, and Calverly couldn't get a clear shot at him. Cassidy shot and missed. Calverly lunged towards the outlaw, pulling the trigger on his weapon as he did. The end of his gun barrel struck Cassidy's forehead, and the bullet dug through his scalp. This enabled Calverly to handcuff Cassidy.

🐞🐞

The Wild Bunch dressed up for what became a famous group photograph, taken in Texas a few months after the Tipton robbery. Unfortunately for the outlaws, the photographer admired their elegance. Proud of his work, he displayed the photo in his store window.

An investigator from the Pinkerton Detective Agency spotted it. His pursuit of the case eventually led to three of the five outlaws being killed. Cassidy and Sundance were thought to have sailed for South America.

The October 31, 1995, issue of the *Casper Star-Tribune* carried an article entitled "Butch Cassidy's Death Still Debated." According to the article, an elderly Rock Springs woman reported that her father saw Cassidy in Rock Springs twenty years after he was supposed to have died in Bolivia.

We may never know what exactly happened to Butch Cassidy, but he did exhibit some good qualities during his criminal life.

In a 1978 issue of the *Newsletter of the National Association and Center for Outlaw and Lawman History,* I. Victor Button recalled an incident that illustrated one of Butch's better characteristics. Button, who was eighty-five when the article was published, said that the outlaws had camped near the Winnemucca, Nevada, ranch where he lived as a youngster.

At the time, Button was about ten-years-old, and he really liked Cassidy's white horse. The bandit told the child that someday the horse would be his, and he kept his promise.

After the Winnemucca bank robbery, the outlaws and a posse were poised for a shootout. When the posse retreated, Cassidy's bunch changed horses, but Cassidy shouted instructions that the white horse should be given to "the kid at the CS Ranch."

Button stated, "I can only say, that for Butch to remember his promise to a kid when the posse was so close, he could not have been all bad."

Rawlins was originally known as Rawlins Springs. In 1867 General Grenville M. Dodge surveyed a railroad route west from Omaha into the land which would eventually become Wyoming.

Near the place now known as Cheyenne, General John A. Rawlins, Chief of Staff of the United States Army, joined Dodge and the civil engineers.

Further west, they approached the hills near the present site of Rawlins. General Rawlins became thirsty. He wanted a good cold drink of water, which he took from a spring near the base of the hills. He stated that it was the most refreshing drink he'd ever tasted.

If anything was ever named after him, he said, he hoped it would be a spring of water. General Dodge marked the spot on his map, naming it "Rawlins Springs."

The incident was reported by General Dodge in his account of the construction of Union Pacific Railroad.

The community which grew by the side of the spring became known by that name. The town became a division point on the railroad. The name was shortened to Rawlins.

General Rawlins was Secretary of War under President U. S. Grant. As Secretary of War, Rawlins had final decision and approval for the first Brooklyn Bridge. He set its height at 135 feet above water. The bridge was painted with "Rawlins Red," an iron-oxide from the paint mine north of the city of Rawlins.

He died in Washington of consumption on September 6, 1869, and is buried in Arlington National Cemetery.

From the Rawlins-Carbon County Chamber of Commerce

Ella "Cattle Kate" Watson

A YARN TOLD ABOUT ONE of Wyoming's notorious women revolves around a crazy quilt made by C. M. Scribner's wife. Scribner drove the stagecoach in the area around Saratoga and Encampment, Wyoming. He happened to have a female passenger one day. He noticed that a lot of dust was being kicked up behind the stage, saw riders that included lawmen, and wondered why a posse would be following them.

"Ma'am," he said. "There's a posse back there. Could they be after you?"

"Why, yes," she replied. Scribner stopped the stage, and the woman stepped out, catching her scarf on a nail as she departed.

Scribner took the swatch of fabric home, and his wife sewed it into a quilt that's displayed at the Saratoga Museum in Saratoga, Wyoming, today.

The passenger? Cattle Kate, the only woman ever hanged in Wyoming.

Controversy surrounds Cattle Kate and James Averell, her partner in a legendary cattle rustling venture. The couple was lynched near the Sweetwater River on the afternoon of July 20, 1889, by six prominent cattlemen.

Historians have typically characterized her as a woman of ill-repute, but a recent book by George W. Hufsmith, *The Wyoming Lynching of Cattle Kate, 1889,* takes a different point of view, stating that Kate was a good woman caught up in the homesteader-stockman dispute of the time, confused with soiled doves, and unjustly wronged to cover up the lynching.

That view angers some family members of one of the men who participated in the hanging of Cattle Kate and James Averell (spelled Averill in some sources) on the Sweetwater River.

Tom Sun was a respected pioneer in Wyoming who was present at the lynching. Kathleen Sun, the wife of Tom's grandson, said that people who knew anything about the incident never talked about it.

Kathleen feels that the vigilante action occurred partly as a result of people needing to govern themselves, to establish some form of law, in the newly-settled area. During the 1880s, one sheriff was responsible for the entire area which is now Carbon and Natrona counties, making law enforcement almost impossible.

"There was no alternative that they could see," Kathleen Sun said.

She asked her father-in-law, Tom Sun's son, about the hanging of Cattle Kate before he died. Tom Sun, Jr. had been about five-years-old at the time of the hangings. He replied matter-of-factly, "She was stealing cattle and they hung her."

"Tom Sun never denied his participation," Kathleen said.

🦢🦢🦢

THE TRADITIONAL ACCOUNT. The evidence appeared strong against Cattle Kate. The traditional account alleges that she was running a local "hog ranch" to entertain the many cowboys who frequented the area. At the ranch, cowboys sought the services of soiled doves and paid with calves, which were rebranded with Cattle Kate's brand. Most of the time, the calves were driven to another place so that the corral was never too full, which might have fueled suspicion.

Cows are protective of their calves, especially when the young ones aren't yet weaned. And cows will track those calves. The rustling might have continued, but Kate's partner, Jim Averell, shot the mother cows to keep them away from their calves in Kate's corral. Upon discovering cow carcasses, at least one rancher, A.J. Bothwell, began to wonder where his healthy, marketable calves had gone.

The local ranchers decided to do something about the problem, making history when they took the law into their own hands.

🦢🦢🦢

THE COURT RECORDS. Probate court records on file at the Carbon County District Court indicate that Ella Watson died intestate on July 20, 1889. In early August, George W. Durant was appointed administrator of her estate. The probate judge in the case was none other than Fenimore Chatterton.

The court records also show that Watson had filed Homestead Entry #2003 at the United States Land Office, applying for this homestead in Cheyenne on March 24, 1888. The property was located just north of present-day Pathfinder Reservoir, midway between Alcova and Devil's Gate on the Sweetwater River, roughly five miles northeast of Independence Rock. After her death, the property was sold at private sale for the best price.

Durant also stated "deceased was the owner or it is claimed she was the owner of 41 head of live stock at the time of her death.... These were taken by A.J. Bothwell and John Durbin and for these cattle there is now a suit pending in this court to recover the value of said stock."

All of Watson's estate was sold "except sewing machine, trunk and its contents, one breast pin and ear rings, two finger rings, one chain and one pair bracelets." These items were given to her father, Thomas Watson, who had arrived in Rawlins from Kansas.

Thomas Watson also was appointed clerk in the sale of the estate items, which included "eight head of cattle more or less, one horse pony, one side saddle, one pony mare and colt, house and fence, and fifteen chickens." The house and fence sold for thirty-five dollars. Two hundred and twenty feet of lumber was also included.

Durant moved from Wyoming to Utah in early 1891, and he urged his own attorney to remove him as administrator, but received no reply. His suit against Bothwell and Durbin was still pending in May 1893. Durant had also been appointed the administrator of James Averell's estate.

Averell's estate included Homestead Entry #1227 at the United States Land Office in Cheyenne dated February 24, 1886. This property is located about a mile and a half south-southeast, as the crow flies, of the Watson homestead. Averell had apparently built certain water ditches, fences, and improvements on this land but did not make the required proofs. Three irrigation ditches and water claims were also listed in his estate.

He had mortgaged "one log house 16 x 42 with 12 x 14 addition at Sweetwater, Carbon County," along with a mule, a wagon, a set of

double harness, six mattresses and a sixteen-by-twenty-four wall tent
to J.W. Hugus and Company to secure payment of a six hundred
dollar promissory note on April 6, 1887. The mortgaged property
was sold on the courthouse steps on August 19, 1889. At the time,
the amount owing was $430.92 and attorney's fees.

The case that Durant brought against Bothwell and Durbin
stated that Watson had said she owned the forty-one head of cattle
branded LU and that the defendants had rebranded the cattle and
turned them loose on public lands. Judgment of $1,100 was asked.

Statements of witnesses included Charles Buck's, in which he
stated that he helped bury the bodies after the lynching and he was
certain that the bodies were those of James Averell and Ella Watson.
He didn't know who the parties were "who done the hanging."

A statement by Ralph Cole, Averell's nephew, reported that he
had lived in the area since April 1889, and that he had met his
uncle, along with John Durbin, A.J. Bothwell, Robert Connors,
another man, Tom Sun, and another man dressed as a cowboy on
the day of the lynching. Frank Buchanan, who also witnessed the
encounter, followed the party to the mountains where he saw the
same men hanging Averell and Watson.

The suit appears to have just petered out. The Carbon County
Clerk of District Court's offices shows no official settlement on the
docket, but neither is there any continuance of the case.

🐚🐚🐚

HUFSMITH'S ACCOUNT. According to Hufsmith's book, Ellen L. Watson was born to Thomas Lewis Watson and Frances Close Watson on
July 2, 1861, near Arran Lake, Ontario, Canada. Her father served
briefly in a medical unit during the Civil War, but returned to
Canada.

Ellen was the oldest of the couple's ten children. In 1877, the
Watsons moved to Kansas. Though Ellen's father filed to become an
American citizen, her mother did not. They didn't naturalize Ellen,
either, which was, according to Hufsmith, "an oversight which later
caused their daughter a great deal of anguish."

Ellen Watson worked in Smith Center, Kansas, as a cook and
housekeeper when she was sixteen. She married a farmer whose land
was located next to her parents' homestead in 1879.

Ella "Cattle Kate" Watson. (Courtesy Wyoming Division of Cultural Resources)

But Ellen would not remain as Mrs. William A. Pickell very long. She filed for divorce in 1884, having moved across the border to Nebraska to avoid the man, who beat her when he'd been drinking and was rumored to have been unfaithful. The divorce was granted in 1886.

Ellen then traveled west, first to Denver, and then to Cheyenne and Rawlins. She worked at the leading hotel of the day, the Rawlins House, from 1884 to 1886.

Hufsmith makes the case that Ella Watson was an independent woman before her time who homesteaded near Averell in 1886. Her homestead encompassed some prized hay meadow which was part of the public land used by Albert Bothwell. When Bothwell could not scare her away, he gathered some fellow cattlemen and, with the help of liquor, lynched her and her trouble-causing friend Averell.

Averell had raised the ire of the cattlemen by uniting home-steaders against the cattlemen and by writing letter advocating the establishment of Natrona County, where homesteaders would have more say in government. His death was not lamented by the establishment.

But what could possibly justify the lynching? The men played on the suspicion that already existed: homesteaders rustled cattle. It was easy for many to believe that Averell and Watson were rustlers.

And that was reason enough to hang a man. But would it justify hanging a woman? They added the accusation which has been successfully used against uppity women for centuries: she was a lecherous woman, a prostitute.

Hufsmith contends that "editorial diatribes" against Watson by newspapermen Ed Towse and Ed Slack of the *Cheyenne Sun*, published after her death, are not accurate, but rather part of a spin put on the crime to cover it up. Hufsmith also claims that Towse confused Ellen Watson Pickell with Kate Maxwell, a notorious soiled dove from Bessemer Bend, Wyoming. Kate Maxwell was later referred to in the press as "Cattle Kate."

To add to the confusion, an illiterate prostitute named Ella Wilson was injured in a gunfight at Fetterman, Hufsmith says. The doctor who treated her injury reported her as "Ella Watson."

🐝🐝🐝

AIKMAN'S ACCOUNT. Duncan Aikman in the book *Calamity Jane and the Lady Wildcats* tells an almost completely different story. He states that Ella Watson came to what is now known as Carbon County in March 1888. James Averell had set up a small store and saloon on the Sweetwater and served as the postmaster. Averell wanted Watson as a partner, so he could hide his shady dealings behind her skirts.

Ella Watson, Aikman says, had a reputation "such that no ordinary crooked promoter would have cared to use her in any enterprise whatsoever." Averell wanted her to establish a brothel near his business in which he would share the profits. This would enable him to operate his business throughout depressions in the cattle industry, but he had something else in mind.

Rustling increased as the small ranchers and homesteaders took up claims on public lands used as range by the large cattle ranchers. When homesteaders lost cattle, they often blamed the big operators who occupied large areas of the range and took possession of any stray, unbranded calves under the Maverick Law.

"Hence, many of the small ranchers felt almost conscientiously that when they rounded up a few calves or mavericks from the nabobs and used them to stave off both starvation and ejection they were merely taking something which the owners had no right to miss and were otherwise performing a civic duty by redressing the balance of economic justice," Aikman writes.

This "moral alibi for rustling" used by struggling homesteaders also attracted people with less than desirable reputations, who were only too glad to assist.

Aikman believes Averell used his store as a cover to assist some of these efforts, and that the Watson establishment took cattle in trade. By branding the rustled calves as soon as possible and arranging for them to be taken elsewhere, the "hog ranch" became a cattle clearinghouse.

Averell chose Watson because she could keep her mouth shut, and, although the larger cattlemen in the area didn't think much of Averell, Watson was reportedly in love with him.

Aikman describes Watson's appearance in 1888 as "a large brunette, frowzily good-looking woman of about twenty-seven years with a sleepy brown eye which veiled more intelligence and resolution than her outward appearance suggested."

Aikman writes that Averell was an outcast, "and Wyoming respectability was convinced that he was also a murderer and a fugitive from justice."

The rustling plan brought the couple some prosperity. Ellen hoped to acquire enough to settle down as a respectable woman one day. She changed her name to Kate Maxwell to honor an admirer. The nickname, Cattle Kate, soon stuck.

Aikman's account goes on to say that before the summer was over, Cattle Kate's ranch became a recognized "hang-out" for local rustlers and hard characters, which began its demise. Local ranchers banned their respectable cowboys from frequenting the establishment.

Scandals surrounded Averell, who, it was claimed, beat one of Watson's women and threw her outside in the snow. He began living openly with Watson. But Aikman claims that Averell did this for the sake of business and that it really was a one-sided affair of the heart.

To make matters worse, Averell, long a proponent of small homesteaders, had stirred up resentments through letters to local publications pushing against the rights of large cattlemen. His applications for a brand were denied five times by the Carbon County brand committee.

A bad winter in 1888–89 increased the rustling operations, but the couple became more and more reckless as the situation became dangerous. Averell began purchasing land, and Watson began dressing more elegantly.

Secret roundups ranging from Cattle Kate's ranch increased. Averell raided the Bothwell ranch stealing calves and shooting the mother cows, but Bothwell saw the dead cattle and missed the calves—calves he'd noted as especially good ones. He went by Cattle Kate's ranch and identified his calves.

The cattle rustling days of James Averell and Cattle Kate came to a macabre end.

🐞🐞🐞

THE FACTS. While many of the "facts" in the case are wildly divergent, it is known that at least six men participated in the hanging, which took place about five miles from Averell's ranch. The bodies dangled from the limb of a tree on the Sweetwater River until authorities from Casper arrived the next day. Averell and Ella Watson were buried side-by-side near the saloon he had operated.

An inquest was held, naming Tom Sun, A.J. Bothwell, John Durbin, R.M. Galbraith, Bob Connor, E. McLain, and an unknown man, as perpetrators of the gruesome deed.

The accused men were arrested by Carbon County Sheriff Frank Hadsell, taken to Rawlins, and released on five thousand dollar bonds each.

When the grand jury convened in Rawlins in October, Judge Samuel T. Corn of the Territorial Supreme Court presided. A witness to the taking of Watson and Averell, a fourteen-year-old boy, died soon after of Bright's disease. Other witnesses disappeared under mysterious circumstances. The grand jury didn't return a verdict, and the accused men were never brought to trial.

In a 1940 edition of the *Wyoming State Journal,* John Charles Thompson wrote that "Buffalo" Tom Vernon, who eventually became a roper and rider in Buffalo Bill Cody's western show, believed himself to be the son of Averell and Cattle Kate. Vernon's account, which had been published in the magazine *Truth,* stated that Ella Watson and Averell were married and that he was legitimately their son. Vernon characterized Watson as a "virtuous, loyal wife."

Thompson wrote of Vernon's story, "His parents, he sets forth emphatically, were not rustlers but were persecuted by big cattlemen for homesteading on the public domain claimed by the owners of large cattle herds as their grazing ground."

Vernon stated that he watched the hanging and saw the bodies taken down. He was then taken on a ride of several days, shot through the neck and chained in an abandoned dug-out. After being rescued by friendly Indians and living with them for six years, he joined Buffalo Bill's show.

Whatever the true story, whether or not Ella Watson was a virtuous wife or a soiled dove, the name "Cattle Kate" stirs controversy still.

"...The escape of Carlisle and the manner in which he is eluding capture is becoming more baffling every day. The belief in general is that it can't be done, but Carlisle has been and is doing it. His picture has been published in hundreds of papers and people all over the country are familiar with his features, yet he has so far failed to be recognized anywhere."

From the *Rawlins Republican,* November 27, 1919

Bill Carlisle

A SIXTEEN-YEAR-OLD purchased a newspaper to scan the classified ads. Discouraged and just about broke, the young man had already held a few different jobs, from selling papers on the street to working as a cowhand.

He was especially excited today, hoping for some glimmer of activity in the mining industry, which is why he'd come to Denver, Colorado. But it was not to be. The rumor he'd heard about the availability of numerous mining jobs proved untrue.

A man from the newspaper office came out carrying a hollow glass gun, an item that came free with want ads placed. The teenager scraped his pockets and paid the stranger thirty-five cents for the toy.

He planned to fill the barrel with candy and give it to one of his nieces for Christmas. But his future experiences with pistols would not prove nearly as sweet.

The young man was Bill Carlisle. He would later become known as "The White Masked Bandit." Carlisle robbed trains, a white bandana covering the lower part of his face. His crime spree began in 1916, taking him through southern Wyoming and northern Colorado, until 1919 when he committed his last train robbery.

Carbon County residents still remember the notorious robber, including events of his life after he became a changed man. Carlisle wrote his autobiography, *Bill Carlisle, Lone Bandit*, in 1946, and some of the county's residents remember that he held a booksigning when the book was published.

Not only did Carlisle commit the robberies, but he served time in the Wyoming penitentiary, where he was sentenced to life. His sentence later was decreased to fifty years, but Carlisle didn't like it.

He escaped after only three years of incarceration. Newspaper headlines of the time proclaimed that he had "vanished." Carlisle was soon caught again. He remained in prison until he was paroled in 1936.

🐌🐌🐌

Born in York, Pennsylvania, on May 4, 1890, Carlisle was the youngest of five children. His mother died when he was only nine months old. The children lived with relatives and in orphanages after her death. Their father was twenty-three-years older than their mother and in poor health.

In 1905, Carlisle joined the circus, a lifestyle which he stated in his autobiography "from the outside appeared so alluring" but lost its glamorous appeal when seen from the inside.

He began his life of crime in Chicago when he robbed some "railroad bulls" who had tried to prevent him from leaving town on a train. From then on, Carlisle wrote, "I was to use all my wits against society."

Carlisle drifted into Wyoming from Denver when the hoped-for mining work didn't pan out. He rode the rails of the Union Pacific from Cheyenne to Rawlins and on to Rock Springs as a stowaway. He looked for jobs in each town, but had no luck. A brief stint in a sheep camp ended with Carlisle again out of work and with only a nickel to his name.

He couldn't find a job in Green River, either. It was cold; Carlisle had endured blizzards and snowstorms throughout his Wyoming travels. Along with his pretend gun, he carried a .32 caliber pocket gun with fourteen cartridges.

He wrote, "You couldn't starve to death in Wyoming if you had a gun with which to shoot game."

And then he had the notion which would set his life into the realm of crime. He could rob the passengers on the train.

On the night of February 9, 1916, Carlisle hid on board Number Eighteen on the eastbound Portland Rose. Around midnight, white bandana covering his lower face and glass pistol in his pocket, he robbed the male passengers and at the first opportunity jumped from the train.

But Carlisle also earned a reputation as a "gentleman" criminal. He apologized for disturbing a woman and child in one of the berths.

The pretend pistol broke when he jumped off the train. Carlisle rolled toward the train's wheels, narrowly escaping death.

He earned $52.35 for his troubles. Soon, the newspapers reported that Carlisle carried a fifteen-hundred-dollar price on his head, dead or alive.

It was the first robbery of its kind in sixteen years.

Three miles from Rock Springs, the bandit followed a trail into the hills, moving constantly to keep from freezing in the frigid air. He laid low throughout several days of frantic searching by law enforcement officials, then returned to Green River.

Witnesses couldn't agree on the description of the bandit, creating much frustration for the lawmen.

Carlisle bought a ticket to Laramie and rode away on the train. The White Masked Bandit faded from front page reports but remained a wanted man.

By April, Carlisle, who had been breaking horses at various ranches, decided to leave Wyoming. He boarded the Overland Limited in Cheyenne by swinging onto the rear platform. Placing his white mask over his face, he robbed the male passengers, hoping that he could gain enough from this robbery to travel to Alaska.

The gentleman bandit again didn't take anything belonging to lady passengers. He only took cash and a few selected items of jewelry.

This robbery earned Carlisle $506.07. It was April 4, 1916. The bandit again disappeared from sight.

Descriptions of the robber again differed, but the reward for bringing him in climbed to five thousand dollars. He traveled throughout southern Wyoming, finding lodging at ranches along the way.

Carlisle doubled his money in a blackjack game in Douglas and headed to Casper.

Several men had been jailed along the Union Pacific line, suspected of being the notorious train robber. This fact bothered Bill Carlisle. He didn't think it was right for another man to take his punishment.

He wrote a letter to the *Denver Post,* enclosing a watch chain he'd stolen from a passenger on the Overland Limited and stating that he would hold up another train somewhere west of Laramie. Carlisle signed the letter "White Masked Bandit."

He left Casper and rode the train to Denver, where the newspapers had reported that police would make short work of him if the bandit came to their city. His letter made front page news.

While in Denver, he attended a concert and a baseball game. Carlisle was never recognized. He then rode the train to Greeley to make good on his promise of another hold-up.

By proving that the White Masked Bandit was still at large, Carlisle hoped that the men being held in jail under suspicion of his crimes would be released.

He boarded the Pacific Limited, this time purchasing a ticket to ride from Greeley, Colorado, to Rawlins, Wyoming. When the train stopped briefly at Hanna, Wyoming, Carlisle went to work, unmasked this time.

But this time, when he jumped off the train, he sprained his ankle. It was April 21, 1916, and it would be the last time the bandit would rob a train—at least for three more years. This time, Carlisle came away with $378.50. And this time, he'd pay for his crimes.

Searchers from Rawlins, Cheyenne, and Laramie came to the area by train to find the bandit. This time, the posse caught up with Carlisle. The front-page of the *Denver Post* reported the capture of the White Masked Bandit twelve miles north of Walcott, Wyoming. It also said that Carlisle surrendered rather than kill to get away.

Sheriff Rubie Rivera of Carbon County handcuffed the notorious outlaw, and they traveled to Rawlins. By May 10, 1916, the White Masked Bandit would be sentenced by a jury to life in prison.

The next three years dragged for the prisoner, but he applied for clemency. Carlisle became a model prisoner, working as the bookkeeper of the prison shirt factory. This job enabled him to keep track of shipments to and from the prison.

Carlisle took up hair weaving and braiding, and he later became a talented crochet artist. He created doilies of his own design and sold them.

The Governor did lessen his sentence—from life to fifty years. But it wasn't enough for Carlisle. Carlisle wrote in his autobiography, "The average life-timer does less than fifteen years, but a man with his sentence cut to fifty years will have to do twenty because of the way 'Good-Time' is figured."

Carlisle decided to break out from the bars that held him. He planned how he could escape without anyone helping him. Carlisle hid in special shirt box he'd made just for the occasion. The convict rode away on a truck, unsuspected. He escaped in November 1919.

He again robbed a train. This time, the train was filled with soldiers and sailors on their way home from France and the First World War. The train was only a few miles from Rock River.

But the gentleman bandit let the soldiers keep their money, saying "I would have been over there with you had they let me go."

Carlisle waited a few moments until the train reached the Medicine Bow station. A young passenger pointed a gun at the robber, who knocked it away and caused it to discharge. The bullet hit Carlisle in the hand, lodging in his wrist.

This holdup netted the robber the grand total of $86.40.

Army troops from Fort D. A. Russell in Cheyenne joined in the search this time. Carlisle kept the posse at bay for two weeks, then was captured at a prospector's cabin near Douglas, Wyoming.

They shot him in the chest. This puzzled Carlisle, who'd been unarmed and had raised his hands in the air. He looked at the event from the human perspective; the lawmen obviously considered him a dangerous escaped convict.

He was taken to the hospital in Douglas, where the doctor operated on his wound. Carlisle spent the next days chained to the bed, and then was moved to the county jail a week later. Another week passed, and then Carlisle was moved to Rawlins.

Thirty-three days after his escape, Carlisle was back in the state penitentiary. He had developed an infection in his wound and was not expected to live. He underwent surgery, a last-chance procedure that might have failed.

But Carlisle was destined to survive, and survival brought an attitude change. He met Reverend Gerard Schellinger, a Catholic priest who was the prison's chaplain. Schellinger aided Carlisle in his attempts to seek clemency, but it would not be granted soon.

Instead, Carlisle became the prison librarian and took business correspondence courses. He began receiving "good-time" credit, and eventually earned parole. Carlisle served the final eighteen months of his sentence at the honor farm near Riverton, Wyoming.

Sheriff Rubie Rivera and Bill Carlisle. (Courtesy Carbon County Museum)

On January 8, 1936, Bill became a free man again. His sixteen years of imprisonment gave him a new outlook and "the courage to look forward, not back over the past." His philosophy that man's mind and soul couldn't be imprisoned by walls emerged through his new life.

He traveled to Kemmerer, where his friend, Reverend Schellinger, was then posted. He opened a cigar store and newsstand there. The small business proved sufficient for him, and he began to make new friends.

But Carlisle's health began to fail. He suffered a ruptured appendix and later had to undergo another operation. While he recuperated, Carlisle became friends with the superintendent of the nursing home. Lillian Berquist chatted with him often. She also played the piano.

On December 23, 1936, they married.

Carlisle wrote in his autobiography that he felt he had paid for his wrongdoing. He felt that he had made his own life difficult, having to learn his lessons the hard way.

For about a year after his marriage, Carlisle worked at a filling station in Laramie. In 1937, the *Saratoga Sun* reported Carlisle's lease of the Spring Creek Camp east of Laramie and noted his plans to open "a lunchroom and a filling station" there. Carlisle's autobiography was published in 1946, ten years after his release from prison. He eventually owned a motel and cafe business in Laramie, which he sold in 1956.

Carlisle's wife died in 1962, and he traveled to Coatesville, Pennsylvania, where he lived with his niece. He died of cancer on June 19, 1964, at the age of seventy-four.

Bill Carlisle became an example of how people can change and learn and grow. Though his life was hard, he paid his debt to society and began a new life. He wrote, "After all, life is like a poker game. If you draw a bad hand, discard it and draw to a better one!"

The site of what would become the future town of Saratoga only contained about three log structures in 1877. William Cadwell and William Brauer chose to settle near the hot springs, an area that local Indians had chosen as a peaceful meeting place. They named the site Warm Springs.

The Indians called it "place of the miraculous waters in the rock" and were spooked away when, during the small pox epidemic of 1874, they tried a tragic cure. To treat the small pox plaguing them, the Indians first dipped themselves, hanging from a pole, into the hot mineral springs to "boil out" the disease. Then the pole was swung around and the Indian was rinsed in the cold waters of the North Platte Rivers. Nearly every Indian who tried this "cure" died, and the Indians from then on considered the hot springs "bad medicine."

Saratoga earned its current name from Fenimore Chatterton, who named it for the resort town of Saratoga Springs, New York, in 1884. The town was platted in 1885, and still contains a street named for Chatterton.

From *The Recollections of Taylor Pennock, Annals of Wyoming,*
Vol. 6 No. 1 and 2, July/October, 1929, and
Tough Country by Gay Day Alcorn

Rubie Rivera

RUBIE RIVERA GAINED fame in Carbon County and throughout the country as the man who brought in the train robber Bill Carlisle. Since its founding, Carbon County had presented many challenges to law enforcement officials, and it wasn't any easier when Rivera was elected sheriff in 1912. However, he earned a reputation for fairness and justice and, though he handled some of the roughest characters, Rivera was never injured in the line of duty.

Things had not been going well in the sheriff's office in the spring of 1916. Rivera's cousin, Jim Hetzler, served as his jailor. Rivera had cautioned him not to trust the prisoners, but Hetzler "allowed them privileges he should never have done," according to Rivera's unpublished manuscript, "Memories," kept at the Carbon County Museum in Rawlins.

Hetzler locked the "trustees" or trusted prisoners in the cells first, saving the most dangerous or least-trusted men for last. The inmates decided to overpower Hetzler, steal his keys, and escape from jail. They talked one of the men with a fairly good record into doing the deed.

The prisoners took a three-quarter-inch pipe from the iron bunks and hit the jailor on the head. Hetzler lingered between life and death.

Shortly after this fracas, the phone call came. "The White Masked Bandit," as Carlisle was sometimes called, had robbed passengers on the Number Twenty-One train east of Walcott. Rivera had to gather a posse to search for the gentlemanly outlaw.

This was the bandit's third robbery. To make matters worse, he had written a letter to the *Denver Post* stating that he would rob the

Number Twenty-One somewhere west of Laramie. To prove his identity, the bandit had included a watch chain he'd stolen on a previous train robbery.

Hetzler's brother arrived to stay by the injured man's bedside, and though reluctant to leave his jailor in such a precarious condition, Rivera prepared to track the bandit.

The Union Pacific made available a special train with engine, caboose, and stock car for saddle horses. Carlisle had earned a reputation as the "second Jesse James," and the railroad wanted him stopped.

Rivera left Rawlins with eight men and in half an hour stopped at the Edson Tunnel, where Carlisle had leapt from the train. It was nearly two in the morning. The stock inspector decided against taking the horses through the tunnel in the dark. He and the horses would stay overnight at Walcott while the others searched ahead.

The posse searched for the robber by flashlight. Rivera found Carlisle's tracks. The bandit couldn't be followed using only the light from the flashlights, so the posse came up with another search plan.

Rivera decided to follow the trail himself. Posse members would walk about ten feet apart from one another. When Rivera needed help, he'd call out. This method would prevent everyone from being killed at once and would allow the posse members a chance to catch the criminal.

Carlisle, experienced at avoiding the law, eluded the lawmen through the night, although he had sprained his ankle when he jumped from the train.

Rivera trailed the bandit all night long. He noticed that Carlisle had pulled his shoes off for awhile, but later put them back on.

When daylight came, Rivera decided to walk back to Walcott to get the horses. The other men were to stay in the area and keep on the bandit's trail. If the trail was lost while Rivera was gone, the men were to stay camped there until he returned.

With daylight also came additional lawmen from Laramie and Cheyenne. The search continued until about three in the afternoon.

One of the posse riders whistled, signaling that he'd tracked the bandit and was near to the man. Carlisle surveyed the situation, hoping that he could take the man's horse and escape. But he realized, as another rider came close to his position, that his plans for escape were useless.

Carlisle wrote in his book *Bill Carlisle, Lone Bandit,* that one of the riders planned to shoot him, even though he put his hands in the air and surrendered. The other rider talked him out of it, but they struggled and the man fired a shot anyway. The shot missed Carlisle, but signaled all the posse members to come running.

Sheriff Rivera handcuffed Carlisle. The general manager of the Union Pacific waited in a special car near the Edson Tunnel to take Carlisle to Rawlins.

Carlisle had the loot from the holdup. He'd been caught on the river bottom of the Platte near an abandoned sheep camp. The Union Pacific had offered a sixty-five-hundred-dollar reward for the outlaw, and Rivera earned five hundred. The rest was split among the posse members.

Carlisle wrote in his book that he was handcuffed to Rivera and taken outside, in front of the Rawlins courthouse, the next morning. Several photographs were taken; the next day, postcard-size photos were sold on the street for fifty cents each. Carlisle stated that he did not receive any of the money.

Rivera also escorted the bandit to Cheyenne, where he was tried and convicted. Carlisle was sentenced to life in prison.

Rivera's cousin, Jim Hetzler, who had been injured in the jail just before the sheriff set off to track Carlisle, died from his injuries.

Later, after he left the sheriff's position, Rivera worked for the Union Pacific as a special agent. When Carlisle escaped from the Wyoming State Penitentiary in 1919 by hiding in a shirt box, Rivera had a chance to track him again. But this time someone else brought in the White Masked Bandit.

The Union Pacific had already spent fifteen thousand dollars on Carlisle's capture the first time. The company hoped the state would catch the escaped convict this time. So Rivera entered the manhunt late in the search.

He recalled that Carlisle later told him that he'd nearly stepped on him during the second search. Rivera said, "He was near enough to hear what I said."

❧✿❧

Rubie Rivera came to Wyoming in 1882 from his father's ranch in the Los Angeles, California, area. Until 1890, he worked as a sheepherder, cowboy, and ranch hand.

Rivera recalled herding sheep from Lone Pine, California, to Elk Mountain, Wyoming, in "Memories." Twenty-six-thousand head of sheep were trailed in bands of about three thousand. One wagon and four horses were allotted to the herders of every two bands. Three herders stayed with each band. Rivera walked.

Desert crossings were long, sometimes forty to fifty miles. Rivera said that the sheep "went wild" one night when they smelled moisture. The herd had crossed a seventy-five-mile stretch of the San Antonio Desert, and herders had to quiet them.

The trail drive lasted nearly six months, beginning in March and arriving in Rawlins in September. But trailing the sheep wasn't all hard work.

Rivera recalled playing poker in the shade of the mess wagon. He enjoyed the game, saying that "for a few years after I landed in Wyoming, I thought I was a gambler." Rivera said he gambled all his wages and played fast enough to keep himself broke.

He earned a reputation also as a top cowhand through his quick thinking and ability to handle emergencies.

In 1890, he began working as a jailor for Sheriff Frank Hadsell of Carbon County. Rivera kept his job when, in the next year, Jens Hansen earned election as sheriff. January 1895 brought another new sheriff, Lou Davis, into office. Rivera stayed on until October, when he decided to enter the sheep business. James Hetzler became his partner.

In 1893, Rivera married Ida Hetzler. He purchased a house lot for $140 and made a payment of twenty dollars each month. The couple's four daughters—Ada, Ruth, Bernice, and Carmen—were all born in the house. Their only son, Ramon, was born and died at the courthouse during the Lou Davis administration.

Rivera borrowed money to build on two rooms. The money was borrowed from another notable Rawlins resident—Dr. John Osborne —eight hundred dollars at twelve percent interest, which later was put into the building and loan association.

James Hetzler didn't like ranch work and returned to town. Rivera stuck it out until 1912, when he ran for sheriff himself.

Rivera held office for two terms, serving the county for four years. During this time, he became interested in mining. He called that experience sorrowful, saying "I parted with some cash."

His personal life took some tough turns as well. Rivera's first wife died, and he fell in love with a widow and married her in 1917. His second marriage only lasted five years. In 1925, with the encouragement of his daughter, Rivera wrote "Memories." He also wrote a second manuscript, "Things Worth While I Can Remember During My Life, Both in California and Wyoming."

The descendant of an old Spanish family, Rubie Rivera died December 14, 1933, and is buried in Rawlins. He was sixty-nine. He will always be remembered for capturing Bill Carlisle, but once said that there were a lot of criminals he dreaded more. Carlisle, he said, "was more like a kid showing off."

Copper ore proved important to the founding of the town of Encampment. Tom Sun had helped plat the town in 1896, but the town didn't have its real beginnings until 1897, when Ed Haggarty discovered a copper vein which eventually became the famous Ferris-Haggarty mine.

During those spectacular copper boom days, Encampment contained several hotels, a hospital, and the professional offices of attorneys, assayers, and physicians.

The town also became famous for the architectural wonder of the longest aerial tramway in the world, built to transport copper ore from the mine to the smelter. Two of the tramway towers, complete with ore buckets, remain standing today on the grounds of the Grand Encampment Museum.

Originally incorporated as "Grand Encampment," the town's name was shortened to Encampment when the post office department required towns to have one-word names.

Sources of information: "I Remember: A Girl's Eye View of Early Days in the Rocky Mountains," a manuscript by Lora Webb Nichols; the Grand Encampment Museum; various issues of the *Grand Encampment Herald*

Tom Sun

THE INFLUENCE OF A YOUNG MAN from Vermont still spreads throughout south-central Wyoming. His destiny included becoming one of Wyoming's earliest permanent settlers, platting the town of Grand Encampment, and scouting the area near Fort Fred Steele. His legacy became one of the largest ranches in Wyoming.

The Sun ranch legacy began in 1872, when Tom Sun built his homestead cabin. The cabin is now registered as a National Historic Landmark. The ranch remained in the hands of Sun family members until the mid-1990s and contained an estimated half-million acres, about eighty percent of which was federal land, and the rest deeded acres and state property. In the 1990s, the family divided the ranch into individual units, still in family ownership. At that time, they also made an agreement with the Church of Jesus Christ of Latter Day Saints (LDS) which allows the church to own about 100,000 acres including the land along the Sweetwater River, the Devil's Gate area, and Tom Sun's original cabin. The church operates a religious and historic interpretive center on the property as well as a working cattle ranch.

❦

Young Tom Sun, born in 1846 in Vermont under the name of Tom DeBeau Soleil, ran away from home after his mother died. The eleven-year-old hoped to find his uncle in Montana. The Sun River was named after his uncle, but the young boy didn't locate his relative.

Instead, he befriended a French trapper called Dakota (spelled "Descoteaux" in some sources). Dakota was a trapper in Wyoming in the 1830s. He met young Tom Sun in St. Louis and offered to take him along on his journey. According to Dr. C. G. Coutant in

History of Wyoming from Earliest Known Discoveries, "The lad accepted the kind offer of the big-hearted trapper and from that day the two became inseparable."

Dakota took Sun trapping on rivers and streams, and the young man learned much from his mentor. As he grew, he learned Indian lore from Dakota and how to survive on the plains, skills which would prove useful when he became a government scout.

The Civil War broke out when Sun was still too young for combat. Undaunted, he worked with an army construction crew in Oklahoma. After the war, he traveled westward, trapping on Wyoming streams and in the Rocky Mountain region.

In 1866, Sun, who by then had anglicized his French name, worked as an army scout with another of Carbon County's most prominent settlers—Boney Earnest. The two men were scouts near the site where Fort Fred Steele was later located.

Buffalo Bill Cody wanted the two men to show him how to be a government scout and pony express rider. Under their tutelage, he learned how to survive in the mountains, to understand the Indians, and to protect himself. Buffalo Bill gave Sun a rifle and later gave Mary Agnes Sun, Tom's wife, a handgun from his Wild West Show.

The skills of Boney Earnest and Tom Sun were required also in Yellowstone Country, where an Indian war party was wreaking havoc. They arrived to discover not only the war party but a hunting party which had been attacked by the Indians.

The men were dead; the women had been taken by the Indians. Sun and Earnest crept into Indian camp to free the kidnapped women. They stampeded the Indians' horses to divert attention, and then freed the women, taking them to Fort Benton in Montana.

In 1868, construction began on Fort Fred Steele near the present-day town of Rawlins. The fort would protect the precious new transcontinental railroad as it was built through the territory. Sprague, Davis, and Company contracted to furnish ties for the new railroad, and Tom Sun and Boney Earnest subcontracted with the company. Other workers included E.W. Bennett and George Wright.

With a logging camp composed largely of Frenchmen, Sun and Earnest floated the first ties down river to the fort. Nicknamed "the French Crew," the group gave French Creek its name.

In 1872, Tom Sun built the now-famous cabin, located on the Sweetwater River, less than a mile from Devil's Gate, a deep crevice in rocky cliffs which became a trail landmark for emigrants. Around the cabin Sun put together a ranch which borders four counties—Fremont, Natrona, Carbon, and Sweetwater—and is one of the oldest and largest in Wyoming. The ranch has been continually operated by the family since 1872 and, before the property was split, contained the longest stretch of the Oregon Trail that remained intact.

The ranch carries a nickname derived from the Sun brand. The brand portrays a wagon wheel hub with three spokes, creating an image similar to a setting sun. The "Hub and Spoke" brand immediately brings to mind the Sun Ranch. The Three Dot brand was used by the Sun in the years 1872–1878, and the Dipper brand, a cross with a check like a dipper on its right, was used when the Suns trailed cattle from Oregon to Wyoming.

Candy Moulton, in an article in the *Rawlins Daily Times* Pioneer Section of March 28, 1986, called Sun "a mountain man and hunter at heart and in experience," stating that he was "a logical choice" when Boney Earnest began guiding hunting parties, many consisting of English nobility, throughout the area.

The scouts greeted the hunters at the Rawlins railroad station, headquartering at the spot where Sun built his cabin. Any trophy heads the hunters had were shipped by rail from Rawlins to the East.

One man, Sir John Rae Reid, wanted to see the large herds of cattle and sheep trailing west along the Oregon and Overland Trails. Reid kept a diary, recording the game killed during his hunting expeditions. He discussed going into business with Sun. When Reid returned to England in 1877, he sent the sum of one thousand pounds sterling to Sun for the purchase of cattle.

Edwin C. Johnson, another hunter, invested in the Sun business in 1878, but their partnership dissolved in the early 1890s. Johnson was anxious to sell the cattle so he could repay his wife the money which he'd borrowed from her. Sun thought cattle prices would increase, and he urged Johnson to wait. Johnson, however, sold the cattle in Chicago for fifteen dollars per head.

Johnson, in his diary which is kept at the Carbon County Museum, recorded that it was a two-day trip from Rawlins to Sun's

Tom Sun. (Courtesy Kathleen Sun Collection)

cabin, a distance of sixty-five miles across "prairie covered with ante-lope and wild geese."

He also recalled killing a grizzly bear, which had partially eaten the elk carcass the hunters had left hanging in a tree. The grizzly was large, and Johnson said it took two men two hours to skin the animal. The bear skin was made into a robe.

Sun traveled to Oregon three different years to buy cattle for his herd, bringing back about two thousand head each time. The cattle were Hereford-Shorthorn crosses. In later years, the Sun Ranch became known for its Hereford cattle.

In 1883, Tom Sun married Mary Agnes Hellihan from County Cork, Ireland. Mary Agnes came to Wyoming from Omaha, Nebraska, to visit an aunt, then worked at the Union Pacific's hotel, the Rawlins House, in Rawlins, which was operated by her aunt and uncle, Mr. and Mrs. Larry Hayes.

The Suns had four children—Tom Sun, Jr., Anastatia, Adelaide, and Eva. Tom Sun, Jr., born in 1884, and Anastatia, born in 1886, both contracted scarlet fever and diphtheria while the Suns were in Rawlins. Anastatia died, and Mary Agnes became superstitious about the town. She did not go to Rawlins for several years.

Mary Agnes earned a reputation for a tidy kitchen. She always placed a white linen tablecloth on the table, even when she was feeding working men, according to Kathleen Sun, the wife of Mary Agnes' grandson, John Sun.

The children attended ranch schools and attended high school in Salt Lake City, Utah. Eva died at the age of sixteen from pneumonia.

Although the Suns suffered through many hardships, life was not always so grim.

In 1896, Tom Sun traveled to Encampment and helped lay out the townsite along with his twelve-year-old son, Tom Sun, Jr. The youngster helped survey by dragging the chain, and he also helped out in another, more unusual way. Tom Sun, Jr. tended bar for a local bartender when the proprietor went fishing.

Kathleen laughed as she recalled that story, saying that residents of Encampment often tell her that the town is "not laid out square with the rest of the world."

Kathleen Sun said that Tom Sun, Sr. "had a marvelous sense of humor." He passed his love of practical jokes on to his sons and grandsons, she said. He once staged a pretend hanging to play a trick on emigrants traveling on the trail, but people soon caught on to the prank.

Unfortunately, another hanging, much more somber in nature, will forever be attached to Tom Sun's history. Sun was one of six men named in the lynching of James Averell and Ella "Cattle Kate" Watson on the Sweetwater River in 1889. He never denied his involvement in the incident. After an investigation, no charges were filed, but controversy over the incident still exists. (*see* Cattle Kate chapter.)

Kathleen Sun said that Tom Sun's reputation has been besmirched by some reports of that hanging, but that he is mostly remembered as an honest, level-headed gentleman. Her own grandfather knew Sun and considered him "a fine gentleman." Sun spoke with a heavy French accent through his life.

During the slack years in the cattle business, some ranchers turned to prospecting for gold in the hopes of supplementing their income. Sun prospected at South Pass, Wyoming, filing several claims. He eventually discovered gold in the Seminoe Mountains and later sold his claim for twenty thousand dollars.

Sun also earned a reputation as a man who would not kill a rattlesnake. He was traveling alone through the Sand Creek area once, and the area was infested with the pesky reptiles. He turned around and went away, later learning that an Indian encampment was on the other side of the creek. Had not the rattlesnakes provided a deterrent, he would have ridden into the midst of the Indian camp, a dangerous situation.

Tom Sun, Sr., the man with penetrating black eyes and a strong sense of humor, died in 1909, and Tom Sun, Jr. took over operations of the ranch. The *Rawlins Daily Times*, in its 1983 Fair Edition, called the elder Sun "one of the most respected and best-liked residents of the Sweetwater section."

In 1924, the ranch flooded, due to an unusual ice jam in the Sweetwater River. Mary Agnes lost many of her treasured possessions to the flood, the only one recorded in that area. She died in 1936.

The Sun family donated numerous items, collected since the 1930s, to the Carbon County Museum in 1983. The family's collection began in 1938 when a fireplace made with rocks from the area was built in the Sun ranch house. The items were previously displayed at the ranch house.

The collection includes a spinning wheel brought from Ireland, pieces of china that Mary Agnes collected from area ranchers, an arrowhead collection, and the rifle Buffalo Bill gave to Mary Agnes.

The Sun Ranch, built by a man who ran away from home as a boy, stands today as his legacy. The ranch is well into its second century of operation with Sun family members at the helm. The ranching operation earned the National Honor Award from the Soil and Water Conservation Society and the annual grazing award from the Wyoming Society of Range Management in 1994. Dennis Sun, a great-grandson of Tom Sun, Sr., earned honors in 1987, chosen as Landowner of the Year by the Wyoming Wildlife Federation and as Citizen of the Year by Wyoming Agriculture in 1992.

The Church of Jesus Christ of Latter Day Saints plans to protect the historical resources on the ranch and used the area in conjunction with its celebration the 150th anniversary of the Mormon Trail in 1997. The portion of the ranch acquired by the church includes Martin's Cove, the area where the Martin Handcart Company took refuge in 1856 when they were caught in an October blizzard. One hundred fifty people died in that tragedy; more than 425 were saved when rescue wagons from Salt Lake City arrived with food and clothing. An interpretive center on the ranch and the Sun cabin are open to the public.

Benton was an end-of-the-tracks town on the steadily advancing Union Pacific Railroad in 1868. Its short life, three months, was due in part to the fact that Rawlins Springs (later called Rawlins) was chosen as the railroad's division point.

A tent town, Benton had a poor reputation. A murder every day and other skullduggery found its way to the town, which also hosted the Big Tent, a saloon and gambling place which came from Julesburg, Colorado, and moved from town to town as the railroad progressed.

Nothing but broken bits of glass, nails, and alkali amidst the sagebrush remains of Benton today. The townsite is not far from the old Lincoln Highway and is located on private property.

Sources of information: *Ghost Towns of Wyoming* by Mary Lou Pence and Lola Homsher; Saratoga Historical and Cultural Association annual trek of 1994

William L. Kuykendall

AN INCIDENT IN THE LIFE of William L. Kuykendall gained him notoriety and illustrates that, in spite of a few well-known incidents of vigilante justice, law enforcement and the judicial system were surprisingly effective in the frontier west.

Kuykendall was selected a judge in 1876 in Deadwood, South Dakota, in a case involving a murder. At the time, the laws to guide his decision were sparse. Only California and Montana had set precedents in a case such as was set before him.

The businessmen and miners in the Black Hills town sought Kuykendall's insight to see justice served. A jury was selected, but they failed to convict the prisoner. Kuykendall had to set the man free.

The prisoner was Jack McCall. The crime? The murder of Wild Bill Hickok.

The unlucky poker hand Wild Bill held when Jack McCall shot him in the back—eights and black aces—became known as the "deadman's hand." McCall's hand in life proved equally unlucky. He was later re-tried in Yankton, South Dakota, convicted, and hanged.

Judge Kuykendall and his wife, Eliza Montgomery Kuykendall, became two of Wyoming's prominent pioneer residents. They lived in Cheyenne before Wyoming Territory was formed, and Eliza's brand, the Rolling M, became the first brand recorded in the territory. Kuykendall served as the first secretary for the powerful Wyoming Stock Growers Association.

❧❧❧

Kuykendall was born December 13, 1835, in Clay County, Missouri. He came to Wyoming thirty years later. The Wyoming

161

population at that time numbered about two hundred, excluding Indians and soldiers.

Kuykendall's enjoyment of law might have been passed down through his family. His father, James K. Kuykendall, practiced law and became the first judge of Platte County, Missouri. Later, he served as sheriff, county treasurer, and judge of probate. In the race for probate judge, he defeated a man named J. W. Denver, for whom Denver, Colorado, is named.

Young William accepted an appointment as deputy clerk of the Platte County circuit court at seventeen. He later became the first county clerk of Jackson County, Kansas. He also served in the office of deputy clerk of the district court of the First Judicial District of Kansas.

During the Civil War, William enlisted as a private in the Fourth Regiment of the Fifth Division of the Confederate Army. He achieved the rank of Captain.

The Kuykendalls were married on July 14, 1857. Eliza Montgomery's heritage dated back to William the Conqueror. William Kuykendall's great-grandfather emigrated to South Carolina from Holland in the 1700s. Both William and Eliza were educated in the south.

The Kuykendalls had four sons, but only John M. and Harry L. survived to adulthood. James died while an infant; William Arthur was killed in Cheyenne in 1878 in an accident with his horse.

Kuykendall traveled to Denver after the Civil War. In the years 1866–67 he built forts for the government in Wyoming, once securing a bid on a contract to deliver two thousand cords of wood by bidding only one cent less than the nearest competitor.

In 1868, he began what would become a very active political career, both in territorial and state politics. The first regular election for county officers of Laramie County, Dakota Territory, was held in October 1868, and Kuykendall was a candidate for Judge of Probate Court. He visited Benton, the "hell-on-wheels" town at the end of the transcontinental railroad tracks, "as every candidate had to do if he expected to be elected to an office in Laramie County," Kuykendall wrote in his book, *Frontier Days*.

Candidates traveled to Benton because of the numerous votes that existed in the short-lived town. Kuykendall called the end-of-

Judge W.L. Kuykendall. (Courtesy Wyoming Division of Cultural Resources)

the-tracks town "probably nearer in a repetition of Sodom and Gomorrah than any other place in America."

Kuykendall recalled that the railroad had just been completed to Rawlins, which was itself just a tent town on the south side of the tracks. He said that "political campaigning along the road to Rawlins was no joke. It was a thing never forgotten by those participating."

All manner of folks followed the westward path of the railroad's construction, including "undesirables." So the campaign trail from Benton to Rawlins undoubtedly provided its share of colorful potential voters. For all the political power held there, Benton lasted only a few months as a town. Now the townsite is located on private property. The alkali flat where a town stood in 1868 contains only bits of broken glass and nails which suggest its existence.

Kuykendall's campaign swing through Laramie, Benton and Rawlins paid off, though. He won the election by a wide margin. He wrote that "friends of other days" helped make his campaign easier in Benton and Rawlins. "Few if any candidates ever knew that such friendships of other days and far different environment were the main factors in causing the result."

In 1870, Kuykendall organized a prospecting expedition for miners, traveling to the Big Horn Mountains in hopes of finding gold. The expedition was dangerous because the terms of the 1868 Sioux treaty forbade white men to travel north of the North Platte River unless they were granted permission by the Indians. But gold fever proved stronger than treaty terms. It overrode even an order from the President of the United States.

Defying the Sioux Indians and the United States government, Kuykendall's group traveled forward. President Grant issued an order forbidding the expedition, but 130 men, prepared for Indian attack, traveled into the area through Camp Brown, located at the present site of Lander.

Indians gathered around them when they reached the Sweetwater River but didn't attack. The area near the Wind River was still basically a wilderness, with sagebrush reportedly growing to heights of seven or eight feet with stems six inches in diameter. The miners prospected near what is the present site of Meeteetse but did not find gold. Near the headwaters of the Wood River, two troops of cavalry intercepted the expedition.

Firmly reminded of the president's order forbidding such a trip, the miners were escorted to Camp Stambaugh near South Pass.

John Henry, one of the men with the expedition, left the group to hunt buffalo and was found dead several days later. The men never knew whether he died during an Indian attack or from a buffalo goring him. John Henry's grave stood near the Wood River Bridge, marked with only his name. In 1911, Kuykendall visited a fraternal organization in Basin. While there he arranged for a more appropriate headstone to be placed on the grave, with an inscription commemorating Henry's participation in Kuykendall's Big Horn expedition.

When the 1870 expedition disbanded, several men traveled on to Montana and others returned to their homes. The expedition broke the ice for other miners to travel through Indian country, and within a few years, gold miners flocked to the area.

After the expedition, Kuykendall served as county treasurer in Cheyenne. He held office as an ex-officio justice of the peace until 1874. Then Kuykendall served in the legislature.

In 1876, he traveled to the Black Hills, where he held a seat in the legislature of Dakota Territory for the four-and-one-half years he lived there. It was during this time that he was chosen to preside over the case of Wild Bill Hickok's murderer.

When he returned to Cheyenne, he became the city clerk there, remaining in that position for three years. He also helped build Wyoming's educational system.

In 1882, he purchased, with his sons, the W. W. Chapman ranch near Warm Springs (Saratoga). This purchase, according to Gay Day Alcorn in her book, *Tough Country*, included 1,272 head of cattle, thirteen head of horses, two wagons with harness, and all improvements.

The ranch business grew. The Kuykendalls, operating as the H Bar, purchased the Swan and Nichols herds in Grand Encampment, cattle from Wagners at Spring Creek, and other stock from Hugus and Mullison at Warm Springs. The Swan herd was purchased for $18,500, according to Alcorn.

The H Bar ranching operation grew to include 1,200 acres of land about four miles south of Saratoga and the 2,400 acre Pick Ranch about seven miles north of the town. Most of the land owned was irrigated.

The Kuykendalls applied for territorial water rights in the North Platte River and in Spring Creek. In the summer of 1882, the Kuykendalls made one of the earliest applications recorded, in Kuykendall Ditch Number Two, for two hundred acres.

By the middle 1880s, the Kuykendalls ran seven thousand to eight thousand head of cattle and owned 150 horses. The nearly seven-thousand acres of the ranch land included two thousand cultivated acres with an estimated twenty miles of fence and three miles of irrigation ditches.

Alcorn wrote, "The Judge said, 'When I took charge, the place did not produce 100 tons of hay. In three or four years it produced from five to seven hundred tons, besides a good acreage of oats.'"

Along with his talents for ranching, Judge Kuykendall enjoyed horses. His son, John, bought a horse named "Pendennis" from its Wisconsin owner, Jerome I. Chase. The judge's brother-in-law, Sam Monroe, served as the trainer. Pendennis, descended from "Merrimac" and a half-brother to "Jay Eye See," was used for breeding. The Kuykendall stable, nearly 160 feet long, included stalls for the horses and enough room for buggies, harnesses, and tack.

The Kuykendalls became well-known for their hospitality, Alcorn reported. One of the sources of entertainment for people in the Saratoga area during the last century was dancing. The great dances were all-night affairs, with guests arriving before dark. Dances like the quadrille were enjoyed until midnight, when supper was served. The fiddlers again took the stage until dawn. After breakfast, the guests returned to their own ranches.

People often traveled thirty miles or more by wagon and in wintry weather to attend the events. Dances at the Kuykendall ranch were noteworthy, along with those held by other settlers of the area, including the Wolfs, Hustons, Monroes, and McPhails.

From 1888 to 1896, Kuykendall served as a member of the Democratic National Committee from Wyoming. He enjoyed membership in several fraternal organizations, including the Odd Fellows, Masons, and Knights of Pythias.

He died in 1915 at the age of eighty. His sons John and Harry published Judge Kuykendall's book, a memoir of his life in the West, in 1917.

'Gee-String' Jack Fulkerson

ONE OF THE TRUE TREASURES left by Jack Fulkerson that his great-niece Lynn Finney still possesses is a copy of *The Marked New Testament* with a handwritten message from a passenger who traveled from Cripple Creek to Colorado Springs on the stage which Jack drove.

The message reads as follows:

To Mr. Fulkerson: who so carefully drove the stage July 29, 1899 from Cripple Creek to Colorado Springs.

I know you have found and will find many dangerous roads and slippery places, as you go through life and I send you this little book that it may keep you safe through your journey as you cared for us, that one rainy day. May God Bless and keep you is the wish and prayer of your friend
M. F. Burrusa, Carrollton, Illinois.

As the message attests, life as a stage driver or a freight hauler was not easy. Finney said that though she didn't remember her great-uncle talking about it much, she knew that his travels could not have all been pleasant and that there were bound to have been break-downs.

Jack Fulkerson was Lynn Finney's "uncle by proxy." He married her grandmother's sister, Lenora "Lena" Porter. He hauled freight from Walcott Junction to Encampment and from the smelter to the Ferris-Haggarty mine. He and Lena later ran the Bohn Hotel in Encampment.

Jack earned his nickname, "Gee-String," through his work. Most drivers use two lines to drive a team of horses, and those lines are known as the "gee" and the "haw" strings. Jack, for reasons only he knew, drove with one hand, using only the right or gee string.

"Gee-String" Jack Fulkerson at the Bohn Hotel in Encampment, Wyoming.
(Courtesy Lynn Finney, Encampment, Wyoming)

Finney said that she wished she could remember more about her great-uncle, but she was a young child when he was living, so most of her memories are happy childhood recollections.

The Fulkersons lived across the alley from Lynn's parents, and Lynn recalled frequently running away to their house when she was only three or four years of age.

Her mother often followed with a switch, but the little girl found the way from Aunt Lena's kitchen to the pantry, which was always stocked with a barrel of molasses or honey cookies.

Lynn's memories focus on Gee-String's twinkling blue eyes, handlebar mustache, and gnarled hands. He drank his coffee from a mustache cup, she said, and always had biscuits and coffee for breakfast. He'd crumble the biscuits into the saucer, then pour coffee over them. And then, he would lift the saucer to his lips and drink from it, to the delight of his young great-niece, who wished she could do that!

He'd also let her sit with him in his easy chair and recliner made of horse hair. Lynn remembers climbing into his lap and sitting with him in the chair. The little girl was also allowed to work the hinges on the chair.

In addition to his sweet side, Gee-String also had a tough aspect. Lynn said that he "cussed like a trooper." The freighter didn't mince words, and he was one tough fellow, as a couple of episodes in his life illustrate.

"He always took very good care of his stock," Lynn recalled. "He treated his horses and mules very well."

One time, when he hauled a load of explosives to the Ferris-Haggarty mine, he arrived after dark. He wanted to take care of his livestock, Lynn said, and to unhitch them. But the men at the mine were eating their meal. They wouldn't help him unload until they had finished eating. Undaunted, Jack returned to his wagon.

"He wanted to do it," Lynn recalled, "and he didn't make any beans about it. He tossed the dynamite off."

Meal forgotten, the miners came running to help after Gee-String had unloaded the seventh box.

Gee-String is also at the center of a local "fish tale," according to R. Richard Perue, who produces historical photographic reproductions in Saratoga, Wyoming, and is a former mayor of the town. Perue said that the fictional tale is really a combination of two stories—a yarn and the story of Gee-String's impatience at the mine as related above.

According to the tale, Gee-String often stopped at the saloon on the east side of the Saratoga bridge, and on one occasion, he was delivering supplies. Again, the story illustrates his impatience. When no one came out to help, he drove his team and wagon onto the bridge, where he threw lighted sticks of dynamite into the North Platte River.

It "blasted water all over and also fish all over Main Street," Perue said.

This may be the source of Saratoga's slogan, "where the trout leap in Main Street," although Irving S. Cobb, a writer of the 1800s is sometimes also credited, Perue said. Cobb said that Saratoga was "where the fish jump," according to Perue.

A poem by Orlando Peterson, Gee-String's brother-in-law, says much about the culture and lifestyle of those early settlers:

"O you old Wyoming, I love thy mountains rough,
Tho' how often have I cussed thee over trails that sure were tough,
Across thy hills of drifted snow, in storms, friend, hard to beat.
With many a pack upon my back, and snowshoes on my feet.
I can tell you hard luck stories of trying "to strike the pay,"
That will never leave my memory if I live till judgment day.
Of the feasts and famines I have seen, say some of 'em were great!
I never missed a meal, pard, tho I've sure sometimes been late.
I've eaten bacon, ham, and bacon till I'd grunt at night in my dream,
I've drunk case after case of cow juice, canned "Evaporated Cream."
I've eaten tons of sour-dough mixings, had the nerve to call it bread.
Compared to Mother's biscuits it's a wonder I ain't dead!
I have blasted at thy mountains till the echoes mocked a roar,
"Keep on drilling here old timer, it is just a few feet more."
I have gone to bed a millionaire, when signs were looking bright,
And dreamt I was a pauper and woke up to find it right.
And back again I've gone, after breakfasting on beans,
Say pard, I'll pull the curtain here on these hard, heartfelt scenes.
But for all our trials and hardships, there's some pleasure just the same.
It's a free and independent life, this old prospecting game.
And it's worth a heap of hardships to be free from other care
At some cabin 'mong the pine trees, in cool, pure mountain air.
Where the summers never get too hot and the nights are always cool.
Where the "Speckled Beauties" frolic in each crystal silver spool.
And tho' I may never strike it, I won't say that I have lost,
When it comes to real dead reckoning why the game is worth the cost.
And when we cross the "Big Divide" and reach that promised land
Where the streets are paved with solid gold and walls of jasper stand,
You may think at last we've struck it, have fulfilled our every wish.
"No, not till we find the River Jordan, and just camp out and fish!"

Another episode in Gee-String's life involved a gunfight in Encampment. Candy Moulton, writing in the book *Saratoga & Encampment, Wyoming: An Album of Family Histories,* quotes Garrett Price's story about Gee-String.

According to the story, Gee-String worked as a bartender in Cluffs. He thought one of the customers, Walt French, had had enough to

1941, Gee-String and Lena Fulkerson holding Lynn Phillips Finney. (Courtesy Lynn Finney, Encampment, Wyoming)

drink that night. Gee-String Jack made him leave the saloon. Price stated, "About 15 minutes after this, as Jack was bending to draw a stein of beer from the barrel which rested on its side, a bullet came through the window. It went into the beer barrel an inch over Jack's head and a stream of beer hit him in the face."

French was arrested and then acquitted, but the day after the trial, Gee-String "caught Walt on Main Street and gave him an unmerciful beating," Price said. "When Charlie Taylor, the marshal, started to interfere, Jack drew his gun and waved the marshal off. Apparently, Charlie did not think that Walt's welfare was worth a gun battle."

Lynn's father, Vern Phillips, remembered that Gee-String loved to greet him at the Bohn Hotel and tell him stories. One of the stories involved a fight Gee-String had. Phillips recalled Gee-String saying that he "took this old rack of bones and I hit him with this one and then I hit him with that one, then I knocked him down and I kicked him in the face, and where his nose was it was just two holes." Phillips said that Gee-String told him that he "tried to kick his goddamn head off."

He didn't look for fights, but he certainly didn't back away from them. Vern said he didn't think that Gee-String missed any fights.

When the flu struck the tiny mining towns one winter, Gee-String hauled the bodies away. Moulton wrote, "Many people died from the virus and were stacked outside in frozen piles at the mining camps. Gee String helped bring the bodies out of the mountains, stacked on wagons like cord wood."

In happier times shown by photographs that Lynn still cherishes, Fulkerson is always dressed sharply, often in a suit and tie. He's shown this way in a hunting photograph taken of Lena and him, while sitting in a chair at the Bohn Hotel, and in front of their home in Encampment. She attributed his snappy attire to his work in running the hotel, though it may have also been a sign of the times. Pioneers often dressed up to be photographed in those days.

Also in those years when Encampment was booming, an opera house operated there. Lynn speculates that everyone dressed up to attend events at the opera house, which is now Encampment's Town Hall.

The Fulkersons ran the Bohn Hotel throughout the 1930s. Lynn also has a book that belonged to Lena Fulkerson which contains detailed information on women and childbirth. The inscription is dated 1907. Lynn said that several people have mentioned to her that Lena was a midwife. Perhaps the book supports their memories.

The couple had lived on a homestead which contained a sawmill prior to running the hotel, Lynn said, though she didn't know if Gee-String ran the sawmill or not.

Gee-String was born on March 29, 1860, and he died at the age of eighty-five. Gee-String Jack Fulkerson is buried in Encampment, where most of his life was spent. "He was meant for this country out here," Lynn said.

Lora Webb Nichols

FROM THE TIME SHE WAS thirteen years old, Lora Webb Nichols kept a diary. Her faithful writing continued until her death, creating a lasting legacy. Her diaries, plus an uncompleted book-length manuscript entitled "I Remember: A Girl's Eye View of Early Days in the Rocky Mountains," provide not only a glimpse of her personality but a snapshot of life around Encampment, Wyoming, as well.

And snapshot is an apt word because Lora also enjoyed photography immensely. Her love of the camera was inspired when she received her first camera at the age of sixteen from her boyfriend, Bert Oldman. She eventually ran her own photography studio.

Lora's writings are kept at the Grand Encampment Museum in Encampment; indeed, her items sparked the museum's very beginnings. The American Heritage Center at the University of Wyoming in Laramie also has copies of Lora's works. Her works were recently compiled into a book entitled, *Lora Webb Nichols: Homesteader's Daughter, Miner's Bride*, edited by Nancy F. Anderson.

According to Anderson, Lora cataloged each photograph and negative, taking care to record the time, place, and content of each one. Her negative file consists of about eighteen thousand entries, including not only her own works but those of others, too.

If she loved to write and photograph, Lora also loved to read. Anderson wrote that along with Lora's favored collection of the *Grand Encampment Herald*, she also had an "extensive library, which included Twain and Dickens, Emerson, ancient and modern classics, westerns, popular fiction, and a nonfiction collection of myriad subjects. Lora read them all and quoted many. It became her habit to mark favorite passages with an *L* at the beginning and an *N* at the ending, forever personalizing her volumes for any future reader."

Lora Webb Nichols was born in Boulder, Colorado, in 1883 to Horace and Sylvia Nichols. Her father, she wrote in "I Remember," liked to name his children after his favorite people. Her brother, Guy, was named for a favorite uncle and a childhood friend; her sister, Lizzie, was named for her grandmother.

But Lora came by her name in a more unusual way. Her father worked as a guard at the Colorado State Penitentiary prior to her birth. The guards walked a beat between two towers, where boxes were stacked to provide a place to sit and rest between walks. It was from one of these boxes, one that had contained Colorado Best laundry soap, that Lora's father came up with her name.

The box was worn, leaving only the letters LORA. Her father thought that would be a pretty name for a girl. Her middle name, Webb, came from a family friend who taught in the Boulder schools.

The Nichols family moved to Wyoming when Lora was just six, using a team and wagon to haul their things.

Lora wrote in "I Remember": "As I try to cast my adult eye back over those years of the late 1880's, I'd say that my parents and their friends and neighbors lived a really rugged life as they established themselves homes and began accumulating stock, machinery, even a few bits of furniture! Always there was the dream ahead, and the rigorous winters, unavoidable illness or accident, were just something to be met and conquered as they came. As a child though I was conscious only of the warm enfolding love surrounding me, and had no feeling of fear or worry."

Lora recalled winter evenings spent reading by the fireside and playing with dolls and doll furniture her dad had made. The family also played games like cribbage and High Five. She wrote that she didn't realize that the cribbage games were really arithmetic lessons in disguise until she had grown up.

Her parents often read aloud, taking turns at each chapter. Especially cherished was a "full set paper bound" of Dickens's work, which Lora's father saved from someone who had planned to throw it away.

"A set of Dickens was like a gold mine to my parents," Lora wrote.

Lora recalled the social activities in the area through her memoir, too. Area ranchers held special dances after the cattle had been gathered in the fall. The all-night events included plenty of food and music.

Lora's memories include being "bundled into the bed of the wagon-box, on a good layer of hay, with quilts spread over it." Leaving home before dark, the families would arrive at their hosts' homes and stay for breakfast.

"Everyone who had a portable musical instrument brought it along," Lora wrote, "...and any person with a talent was called on always." She felt that her father was one of the best tap-dancers around, and he also had a flute and a five-stringed banjo. Lora's sister played the banjo and violin, and both men and women sang or even read aloud during the festivities. After 1897, when the town of Encampment was established, Lora wrote that more pianos were in evidence.

Schools were scarce, however. Lora and her sister attended the school taught by Mr. Wolfard in a schoolhouse built four miles from her family's homestead. Though Lora's mother was also a qualified teacher, she did not feel her efforts at teaching her daughters were satisfactory. And although Lora first attended school at age eight, riding with her sister on their gentle bay mare, Bess, the weather proved too unstable. One teacher, William Platt, often visited the Nichols family to help keep the girls current with their schoolwork when blizzards and cold snaps plagued the area.

But Lora's parents felt that just wasn't enough. So important to them was their children's education that they sold their ranch and moved to Colorado in 1893. The cattle sold at twelve dollars per head.

Lora's daughter-in-law, Vera Oldman, wrote in *Saratoga and Encampment, Wyoming: An Album of Family Histories*, that Lora loved horses, beginning with a saddle horse named Nibbs, who was given to her by Joe Letora, a family friend. Other favorites were Comet and Buster. Lora also often mentioned her beloved cat, Yankee, in her diary.

Lora "endured" the four years that the family lived in Colorado, and everyone grew homesick for "the dear old ranch in Wyoming." Though they lived close to Lora's father's parents in Colorado, Lora wrote, "no other place could ever be HOME to any of us."

May 20, 1897, became "a red letter day in our family," she wrote, explaining that the date forever marked "the day we got home." She had begun keeping her diary by this time. Vera wrote, "Her thoughts, her joys, and sorrows are reflected in this diary. So much of Lora will live on forever because the original diary has found its way to the Encampment Museum."

Anderson wrote that Lora used her diary "to ascend to the melodramatic and then dismiss the case" and that the diary had become "the recipient of her wrath and her elation, her every mood recorded in lively, fresh prose."

Many changes had taken place by the time the Nichols family returned to Wyoming. The town of "Grand Encampment City" was being created, and Lora remarked that "the little town grew like a mushroom." Trees, which had previously grown only along the riverbanks, now shaded homes; Encampment was taking on a look of permanence.

Lora married Albert H. Oldman in October 1900 at the home of her parents.

This began her time as a miner's wife, living in many different homes. Vera wrote that Lora's interest in photography grew during this period, too. Bert had given her her first camera, and at age sixteen, Lora took pictures for friends.

Vera wrote, "She took a correspondence course in photography and many pictures of Encampment buildings are a result of that course. She worked at the Smith Studio and learned more. For a short time, she ran the studio on her own. That building stood on the present parking lot at the Masonic Hall [now Freeman Avenue]."

The couple had a son, Bert, Jr., and a daughter, Sylvia, but the marriage was not destined to last. Vera Oldman, who married Bert, Jr., wrote, "Lora loved her children but this marriage did not last. The difference in ages may have been a factor." Lora divorced Albert about 1908.

Love came a second time for Lora, however. In 1914, she married her cousin, Guy H. Nichols, at the courthouse in Walden, Colorado. Four sons were born to this union—Ezra, Clifford, Frank, and Dick. During World War II, all four of the boys served in the armed forces.

Vera reported that Lora always worked, whether she was running the photography studio or publishing the local newspaper, to supplement her family's income. Guy was "all right but a poor provider," Vera said. He was a common laborer and times were hard then.

Of her mother-in-law, Vera said, "I'm glad I knew her. I admired her so much."

Vera recalled her own wedding day. Vera had been teaching school in Encampment for about four years when she and Bert Oldman, Jr., decided to marry. They set their date as the last day of school. They wanted to keep their wedding quiet, so they slipped away to Saratoga on Thursday night. The happy couple stopped along the way to pick up Lora and Guy Nichols who attended the private ceremony. Vera remembered attending the school picnic that Friday and then "slipping away" to honeymoon with her new husband.

"Lora was always so good to me," Vera said. "I have many happy memories of her."

Lora also wrote in "I Remember" about her first time voting in an election. She included the *Grand Encampment Herald's* description of the voting "blunders" made by several of the ladies on that November 1904 day. The mistakes included writing a name on the outside of the ballot and tearing a ballot in two and needing another. The newspaper reported, "... and yet, every vote counted, and the fact is, barring a few incidents as above, the ladies of Encampment showed just as much intelligence with the ballot as the men, and perhaps on the average a little more so."

Lora added her own thoughts, writing, "I cast my own 'first' ballot that year, for 'Teddy' [Roosevelt]: I hope none of the above blunders was made by me...I felt very important, being a voter."

In 1935, Lora moved to Stockton, California, feeling that a lower altitude would help her heart problems. After working at several different jobs, she took a position as the Superintendent of the Stockton Children's Home. Her beloved Encampment still called to her, though, and Lora returned again after she retired. Guy Nichols never left Encampment. He died there in 1955.

Lora died in 1962 from what her daughter-in-law called "a worn-out heart." She is buried in the Mountain View Cemetery near Encampment. "She had touched many lives as she traveled along life's way. She counted many young people as her friends. Life wasn't easy for her, but she lived a life of service," Vera wrote.

Lora's own words may sum it up best. She wrote, "In our short span of life we humans can but take our place in the ever-changing tapestry of life, where the babies are being woven in at one extremity as the old folks are being ravelled out at the other."

Lillian Heath Nelson

LILLIAN HEATH, BORN DECEMBER 29, 1865, to William and Calista Hunter Heath, on her grandfather's farm in Burnett Junction, Wisconsin, journeyed with her family from Wisconsin to Iowa and eventually to Wyoming.

This cross-country journey would lead Lillian to the career path that made her name famous.

The Heaths came from Aplington, Iowa, to Cheyenne, Wyoming, by train. Lillian recalled in a 1961 taped interview on file at the American Heritage Center, University of Wyoming, Laramie, Wyoming, that "Papa got the wanderlust." He traveled to Laramie to find out about homes, entering the employ of the Union Pacific as a baggage man in 1873.

His wife and daughters joined him on the Heaths' tenth wedding anniversary, September 26, 1873. They traveled by train, in a coach with a coal stove in one end providing warmth. In 1877, the Heaths moved to Rawlins, where Mr. Heath worked as a locomotive painter.

In the 1880s, Dr. Thomas Maghee practiced medicine in Rawlins as the Union Pacific physician and surgeon. Dr. Maghee did not live in Rawlins but scheduled regular visits and was called for emergencies and accidents. William Heath often assisted Dr. Maghee and provided on-site medical attention when Dr. Maghee was not in town. The two men, both Civil War veterans, shared an interest in medicine, though Mr. Heath never became a physician.

William Heath brought the stories of his experiences home to his young daughter. "It was not very long before I was head over heels [about medicine]," Lillian said during the taped interview.

Dr. Lillian Heath. (Courtesy Carbon County Museum)

Soon she became "nurse and assistant and errand boy and everything" for Dr. Maghee, helping deliver babies, perform amputations, and fix bullet wounds.

At the insistence of her father and Dr. Maghee, Lillian dressed in boys' clothing. She carried a .32 caliber revolver inside a specially designed jacket. Rawlins was a tough town in those days, and women were not safe on the streets. Her father had Lillian measured for trousers, and she wore a coat and vest and a fur cap, fixing her braids on top of her head. She was never accosted but was always prepared.

One of the cases she assisted Maghee with involved a sheepherder who had failed at his suicide attempt. The man, who had shot himself in the chin, survived with most of his face ripped away. Dr. Maghee and Lillian set to work to restore the man's face—a plastic surgery case, a medical specialty that hadn't yet been named.

The restoration required over thirty surgeries, and Lillian helped with the anesthetic—chloroform. Together, Dr. Maghee and Lillian rebuilt the man's face, feeding him through a tube for several weeks and patching him up, bit by bit, during each operation.

Lillian recalled in a 1955 article in the *Denver Post Empire* magazine that his jawbone grew back by itself, miraculously without infection. Using silver tubes for nostrils and a "keystone of skin" from high on the man's forehead, Dr. Maghee and Lillian fashioned a new nose, leaving the keystone attached at the top for circulation.

"It was a wonderful, wonderful thing, the way the flesh grew and formed," Lillian said in her taped interview. The nose healed with no scars, but the man didn't like his new nose.

"He was a very much better looking man when we finished," she recalled. "He had a fierce, fierce scowl. His eyes would just blaze."

The sheepherder often was found jerking the hairs out of the middle of his nose. He hadn't been thrilled at being found alive. However, after a time, Lillian said, he "finally became amiable to me."

Her appreciation and respect for her mentor, Dr. Maghee, was evident as she related the sheepherder's tale.

"Nobody ever appreciated Dr. Maghee," she said. "He was so versatile and knowledgeable."

Dr. Maghee and Lillian Heath also studied another famous case in Wyoming's history. When Big Nose George was lynched in Rawlins, Maghee claimed the outlaw's body for medical study.

Dr. John E. Osborne, the second medical doctor practicing in Rawlins, skinned the body and had a pair of shoes made from the skin. The doctors also sawed off the top of Big Nose George's skull, hoping to study the differences of a criminal's brain. Lillian took the skull cap, which she kept in her home for many years. In the late 1990s, the outlaw's skull halves were reunited as part of a University of Wyoming study. (*See* chapter on Big Nose George Parrott.)

According to an article published in the *Rawlins Daily Times* at the time of Lillian's death, she said that the skull was still bloody with a piece of hair on it when it was given to her. The skull contained a bullet mark, and it was thick, which indicated "very small mentality." The gray matter could not expand, she explained, because the skull had formed abnormally.

With all these fascinating medical experiences behind her, Lillian eventually had to make a career choice. Medicine wasn't at the top of the list of careers for women in those days.

Lillian began "fitting myself for a teacher," and at the age of sixteen she taught at the Number Five Mine near Carbon, Wyoming, the first Union Pacific coal town in the state. She also taught at the Pass Creek school, located north of Saratoga, and substituted in the Rawlins public school.

In 1886, Lillian graduated from the Rawlins High School at age twenty-one, a member of the second class to graduate from the school. Her interest in medicine remained strong, however. Lillian worked with Dr. Maghee for seven years, and then she attended the University of Colorado in Boulder, Colorado, for one year, studying for her doctorate.

Even though Dr. Elizabeth Blackwell forged the path for women to attend medical school years earlier in 1849, during Lillian Heath's youth it was still difficult for women to gain admission to medical schools. Dr. Maghee's influence helped, as did the steady encouragement of her father.

"My own mother didn't think it was right for me to go to medical school," Lillian recalled in the taped interview. "Papa helped me in every way."

She received her degree on March 7, 1893, from the College of Physicians and Surgeons at Keokuk, Iowa. She was twenty-seven years old.

Only two other woman graduated in the twenty-two student class. Lydia Etta Smith of Placerville, California, and Mary Ellsworth Wilkins of Greenville, Illinois, graduated with Lillian.

Lillian specialized in obstetrics, studying for three more months after graduation. She also worked in the hospital that was operated in connection with the college, a requirement of medical students.

Doug Atterberg of the Lee County (Iowa) Historical Society said that the academic year for the college ran from October through March so that cool weather would help keep the cadavers the medical students studied fresh. The college closed in 1908.

When she returned to Rawlins to set up her own medical practice the summer after she graduated, Lillian Heath, M.D., became the

Dr. Lillian Heath Nelson holding Big Nose George's skull cap. (Courtesy Carbon County Museum)

first woman to practice medicine in Wyoming. She was twenty-seven years old.

She practiced in the Heath home at 111 West Lincoln Way, and her practice was mostly confined to Rawlins. Persons needing medical assistance who lived outside of the town usually came to her because of poor communications systems. However, she recalled occasionally traveling by buckboard or on horseback, sometimes thirty or forty miles, to help patients. She said in the taped interview that she rode a sorrel horse.

She joined the Colorado State Medical Society and kept her membership from 1895–1900. She was the only woman doctor who appeared at the American Medical Association's 1895 convention in Denver, Colorado. There was not yet a Wyoming Medical Society.

She spent time attending summer medical clinics in Denver, enjoying spare time visiting the Daniels and Fishers "French Room." In the department store's French Room, Dr. Heath modeled garments for store personnel. Her clothes needed little adjustment, because she was "a perfect 36" and wore a size two-and-a-half shoe and a size six glove.

Bicycling also interested her, and Lillian Heath was the only woman member of the Rawlins bicycle club in the late 1890s. Her father was also a member of the club.

It wasn't easy being a woman physician in those days. Lillian recalled a woman asking a mutual friend if Lillian knew anything. Lillian's friend replied that she wouldn't have Dr. Heath for her physician if she didn't know anything. The woman apparently said that she expected to employ Dr. Heath but didn't expect to pay her, and Dr. Heath eventually had to tell the woman to find another physician.

Women today often face tough tests in careers previously chosen only by men. However, Lillian said in the taped interview that men were more accepting of her career choice than women.

"Men folks received me cordially. Women were just as catty as they could be," she recalled.

She gained a reputation as "a perfect anesthetist" among the other doctors in the neighboring areas. She "never had a bauble" with the procedure but said that she thought ether was awfully hard to use when it was first being developed. Sometimes it proved effective, and sometimes it didn't, she said.

Prior to ether, chloroform was the anesthetic used. Administering it was a judgment call. Lillian recalled giving a dose of whiskey first, depending upon the size of the individual.

"You have to use your noggin," she said.

Other medications included "every old time memory anybody ever heard of," she said, though Dr. Maghee didn't like to use anything new until he was sure it was safe. Alcohol was used exclusively as an antiseptic, and the drugs morphine, cocaine, and opiates were used as well. Codeine was just coming into use, she said.

She recalled that green soap and lots of hot water were used as precautions. Sulphur, which was blown into the throat with a goose quill, treated numerous ailments including diphtheria.

Eventually, Lillian Heath gained such fame that letters addressed simply to "Dr. Lillian Heath, Wyoming" reached her.

A forerunner of today's career women, who no longer have to make a choice between marriage and career, Lillian Heath chose both and succeeded.

Lillian married Lou J. Nelson, a painter and decorator, in 1898. Mr. Nelson said in the *Empire Magazine* article, "a prettier girl I never saw. I married her quick as I could, in Omaha, Nebraska, where I was stationed with the army in 1898."

Nelson had been stationed at Fort Ord, Nebraska. He was a member of President William McKinley's honor guard when the chief executive attended the Trans-Mississippi Exposition in Omaha.

Lillian wore a full length gown with a white lace robe over layers of white Swiss silk and chiffon at the simple ceremony performed in the home of friends in Omaha.

The couple lived in Rawlins for most of the rest of their married life. During the years 1909–12, they lived in Lamar, Colorado, where they operated the Ben-Mar hotel. Lillian's father, William Heath, died while visiting his daughter and son-in-law in 1911. After her father's death, Lillian's mother lived with the Nelsons until her death in Rawlins in 1930. The Nelsons had no children.

Though she only actively practiced for about fifteen years, Lillian remained interested in the medical profession throughout her life. She met Dr. Elizabeth Blackwell, but her voice was tinged with regret when she recalled that the two women didn't have time to have a full-fledged conversation. Dr. Blackwell's touring schedule was just too hectic. In later years, Dr. Heath flew to Denver to inspect the city's hospitals for a one-day visit. She was eighty-nine at the time.

The *Denver Post* reported that she still read at least six newspapers each day. At the time of her death in 1962 at the age of ninety-six, the *Rawlins Daily Times* wrote that Dr. Heath had remained active in several local organizations along with doing all her own work at home.

Perhaps she summed up her life best in her own words. At the end of the AHC taped interview, Dr. Heath revealed what was already most obvious, "I'm not a quitter."

Frederick Wolf

LADIES ENJOYED DAILY TEAS in the second floor ladies' parlor of the Hotel Wolf, an elegant room decorated with beautiful curtains, luxurious furniture, and heavy Brussels carpeting. The pastries they ate were prepared under the supervision of their hostess, Christina Waldeman Wolf.

Mrs. Wolf had been a cook's pastry apprentice in Germany, work which equipped her with the necessary skills to help her husband, Frederick, at his fine new hotel. It soon became known as one of the best in the country.

Historian Gay Day Alcorn wrote of the hotel in *Tough Country*, "It was often filled from garret to cellar with prospectors, mining men, investors, Eastern gentlemen and ladies on pleasure excursions and fishing trips."

The hotel opened with a special celebration on New Year's Eve of 1893. Saratoga residents celebrated the holiday with a dinner at the Gold Hill House and a masquerade ball at the Hotel Wolf.

The hotel today remains a Saratoga landmark, standing at the corners of First and Bridge Streets. It is listed on the register of National Historic Places.

Current owners Doug and Kathy Campbell celebrated the historic hotel's hundredth year by hosting an event similar to Frederick Wolf's original celebration.

The Campbells feel the hotel was built more with function in mind than with luxury, though it is often described as an elegant place. The hotel served as a stage stop, and Kathy said that travelers on the stage line were probably thrilled with the comfort of the Hotel Wolf.

❧

The man who created the Hotel Wolf, Frederick G. Wolf, was born in Flein, Wurttemberg, Germany, on December 27, 1845. He was the oldest child of Frederick and Margaret (Nebelmesser) Wolf's family of ten. He had worked in his father's occupation, wine gardening, and had served in the German Army before he traveled to the United States. His father had served as the burgomaster for eighteen years and as the revenue officer of the German government, according to a manuscript prepared by Fay Anderson in the 1940s. The Wolf family were prominent residents of the area.

Leaving his fiance, Christina, behind, he arrived in New York City in 1869. Wolf worked later with the Michigan Central Railroad in Michigan City, Indiana. Christina soon followed him to America, and the couple were married on September 11, 1869.

The Wolfs came to Rawlins in 1875. Frederick worked as a foreman with the Union Pacific Railroad. He later entered the liquor business.

He tried ranching, first in 1882 near Lake Creek and then at Brush Creek, about twenty miles southeast of Saratoga. But rheumatism and ranching were not a good match, so Wolf again went into the liquor business.

According to Alcorn, William F. Swan purchased Wolf's ranch and cattle in 1884.

Kathy Campbell researched the hotel's first owner for a Wyoming history class, discovering that Wolf was elected Sergeant-at-Arms of the House of Representatives for one session in Cheyenne. She was not able to confirm that he served in the position, however.

But Wolf eventually found a career which would last. In 1893, the contract was let for a three-story building, forty-two by sixty feet, in Saratoga. The building would eventually bear his name.

Wolf managed the Gold Hill House, which was located across the street from the Hugus Building (on the corner of Bridge and River Streets), until his own hotel was built.

Kreigh and Maddy was awarded the brick contract, and the bricks were made in Saratoga. D.C. Kinnaman of Rawlins served as architect. The first floor contained woodwork made of finely finished Georgia pine, and the luxurious effect was continued in the upstairs ladies' parlor. The cost of building the structure was six thousand dollars.

The masquerade ball and dinner held on December 31, 1893, marked the hotel's opening, but the Hotel Wolf officially opened for business on January 10, 1894. The hotel was billed as a hostelry where "light warmth and comfort everywhere prevails," according to Kathy's research.

The local newspaper, the *Platte Valley Lyre,* carried an enthusiastic report of the celebration which was reprinted in 1993 in the *Saratoga Sun.* The newspaper report described the banquet, held at the Gold Hill House, stating, "The tables literally groaned under their load of good things, and the feast will never be forgotten by those who partook. Long live the Hotel Wolf and its popular landlord!"

Because the new structure was not large enough to hold both the dinner and the dance, only the masquerade ball was held at the new hotel, which was "filled with a merry crowd of dancers and spectators." The *Lyre* stated, "The interior of the building had been tastefully decorated for the occasion with bunting, evergreen trees, and festoons of flowers, and the word 'welcome' appeared in large letters over the archway in the dining room."

Celebrants danced quadrilles and cavorted until four in the morning. The *Lyre* reported, "Landlord Wolf was here, there, and everywhere, his genial face beaming a cordial welcome to every guest."

In July 1894, Wolf opened a sample store with "none but the finest brands of liquors and cigars." The Campbells have worked on restoring the door that led into Wolf's sample room, discovering that underneath the finish, the words "Sample Room" can still be seen. The door leads now into the Saratoga Room.

Alcorn reported that the years from 1888–97 were ones of especially high cultural enjoyment for Saratoga residents. The Wolf daughters worked hard for their church, enjoying the services officiated by Reverend R. E. G. Huntington.

Alcorn wrote that the Huntingtons' daughter Carrie recalled the period by saying, "Saratoga was a nice place to live, with many fine people, bankers, store keepers, two churches, a number of teachers, all of which gave the town a good atmosphere. A library was established and a cultured atmosphere developed that was delightful."

In 1900, after traveling to Florida, the elder Wolf returned to a surprise. His son, Frederick M. Wolf, had wallpapered and painted the entire first floor. The dining room was described as a "poem in green and brown and the most attractive spot to be imagined."

But tragedy was to follow the lovely surprise. Young Frederick drowned in 1901.

Ironically, he had served in Colonel Torrey's Rough Riders during the Spanish-American War with George W. Sisson, a man who would later purchase the Hotel Wolf from Christina in 1935. Sisson also died of drowning, in a fishing accident on the North Platte River.

The hotel was remodeled in 1902, when electricity came. Kathy's research indicated that Wolf leased the hotel to his son-in-law, A.J. Doggett, for a brief time beginning in 1902. Wolf resumed management in 1906.

Progressive Men of Wyoming states, "Mr. Wolf is one of the leading citizens of his section of the state, and has done much to develop its resources and build up its industries, always taking a foremost part in the promotion of every enterprise which is calculated to benefit the public and contributing his time and means to all worthy measures for the good of the community, he stands high in the respect of his neighbors and of all the people of that portion of Wyoming. He has been very successful and is counted one of the solid business men and substantial property owners of Carbon County."

Christina and Frederick Wolf had four children—Carrie, Freida, Frederick M., and Henrietta. Their youngest daughter, "Nettie," suffered from epilepsy.

For a short time, Wolf leased his hotel to Charles E. Shipley. He returned to manage the hotel again, renovating it in 1910.

Frederick G. Wolf died on December 1, 1910.

Willis George Emerson

THE TRAMWAY NO LONGER carries copper ore from the Ferris-Haggarty mine to the smelter in Grand Encampment. Three towers of the now defunct engineering marvel stand at the Grand Encampment Museum, reminders of the days of excitement and hope that characterized the short-lived copper boom.

Emerson Street still runs through the small Wyoming town, and the E & H Building stands at the corner of Sixth and Freeman. Few other reminders of Willis George Emerson's life and work in Encampment are visible, but his influence remains unmistakable.

Willis George Emerson came to the Encampment area in 1897, before the town existed. With his associates Bernard McCaffrey, Charles Freeman, Ed Heizer, and Charles Clemmons, Emerson organized a townsite company. The townsite was platted a mile square, which provided enough room to create a city with four city parks. Each of the parks would surround a small lake.

Lora Webb Nichols, in her manuscript "I Remember," recalled her family's return to Encampment on May 20, 1897, after staying a few years in Colorado. Nichols wrote that a line was being plowed around the townsite, then consisting of one log cabin and a few tents.

"Emerson and his associates were reported as 'smooth a group of promoters and developers as could be found anywhere,' and they lived up to that reputation," she wrote.

Advertising for the copper camp began in the fall of 1897. Emerson, according to the *Grand Encampment Herald*, was a former newspaperman and a member of the Chicago Press Club. He had many friends in business throughout the nation, and he enlisted the promotional help of Grant Jones of Chicago. Jones had contributed to the *Chicago Daily Mail* and the *Chicago Times Herald*.

Historian Mark Junge, in his 1972 booklet, *The Grand Encampment*, wrote, "Optimistic opinions were voiced predicting that Encampment would be the new 'Pittsburgh of the West,' or a second Denver, and the hope was even expressed that the town would serve as the location of the new Wyoming State Capital."

It didn't happen, but the optimistic outlook abounded during Emerson's decade-long stay in Encampment. A decade was also about the life span of the copper boom.

Emerson was born near Blakesburg, Iowa, on March 28, 1866. He graduated from Knox College in Galesburg, Illinois, in 1886, and later received an honorary degree from Northern Ohio University.

He earned admittance to the Iowa State Bar in 1886, then moved to Kansas where he became a banker. He served as a Kansas presidential elector in the Harrison-Norton campaign in 1888. While there he became a York and Scottish Rite Mason.

And Emerson enjoyed writing, specializing in fiction and verse. Before arriving in Engcampment he wrote *Winning Winds* in 1885, *The Fall of Jason* in 1889, and *My Partner and I* in 1892. Emerson continued writing in Encampment, producing *Buell Hampton* in 1902. After he left Wyoming, he published *The Builders* (1905), *The Smoky God* (1908), and *The Treasure of Hidden Valley*, set in Encampment (1915). Emerson wrote two manuscripts that were only partially completed, *The White Wolf* and *Shall the Woman be Stoned*. The manuscripts were under contract with Chicago-based publisher Forbes and Company, for later publication, according to Fay Anderson's Work's Project Administration (WPA) research.

When Emerson came to Wyoming, he began promoting the copper industry. The *Grand Encampment Herald*, the "official newspaper of the Grand Encampment Mining District," reported that 1,033 acres were proven up under the "Placer Act." As a result, prospectors from Colorado, Montana, and Utah invaded the area, looking for their lucky strike of precious metals.

The discovery of a white quartz boulder "shot full of free gold" and weighing about seven or eight tons, created a rush of excitement.

An eastern smelter estimated the value at around seventeen hundred dollars per ton. Though the boulder was discovered in Purgatory Gulch, the mother lode remained "shrouded in mystery," according to the *Herald.*

Gold was not to be the true treasure of the mining district, however. No other significant gold finds were made, but copper abounded.

Newspapers throughout the nation carried advertisements about the area, including the *New York Herald, New York Sun, Philadelphia North American,* and *Atlanta Constitution.* Newspapers in Cleveland, Cincinnati, Pittsburgh, Chicago, Kansas City, Omaha, and Denver gave space to the ads.

Ed Haggarty, soon to be one of Encampment's most "prominent and respected citizens," happened to read a copy of the *New York Herald.* He set off for the Encampment area to search for copper. In 1898, he secured backing from Thomas Deal, J.M. Rumsey, and George Ferris, then filed on the claim called "Rudefeha." The name came from the first two letters of the men's last names. The Rudefeha claim eventually became known as the Ferris-Haggarty mine.

The *Grand Encampment Herald* reported that the mine was "in pay ore almost from its grass roots." Several thousands of dollars of high grade ore was mined from 1899–1901 and hauled sixty miles by wagon to ship to Colorado and Chicago smelters by rail.

In January 1899, Willis George Emerson and Bernard McCaffrey invested in the company, and it became known as the Ferris-Haggarty Copper Mining Company. Rumsey sold his interest first for one thousand dollars. Then, Haggarty sold his initial interest to George Ferris for thirty thousand dollars. That summer Ferris was killed in a wagon accident; his widow Julia acquired his interest. Additional investors had joined in the company by this time.

In 1901, rumors crept up that the company would consolidate with Battle Lake mining operations, but the *Saratoga Sun* quoted I.C. Miller of the Ferris-Haggarty Mining Company, "There is absolutely no truth whatever in the rumored consolidation of the Rudefeha with other Battle Lake properties. We have too good of a mine to ever think of such a thing as that. We could not afford to pool the interest of the Rudefeha with a mine of lower grade ore whose development and facilities were not as good as ours."

In October 1901, Emerson received a contract from the Ferris-Haggarty Mining Company to construct an aerial tramway. The tramway's purpose was to bring ore from the mine to the smelter in Grand Encampment.

The *Herald* reported, "The signing of this contract changed the map politically and otherwise of the State of Wyoming."

Other ideas, such as building a railroad, had been discouraged because of the mountainous terrain and the heavy winter snows in the area.

Emerson decided that the only possible solution was the tramway. The result, a sixteen-and-a-half-mile aerial tramway, the longest in the world, attracted the curiosity of engineers throughout the nation, the *Herald* reported. Construction of the tramway cost an astounding sum of $365,000.

In September 1902, before the tramway was completed, the North American Copper Company, organized under the laws of New Jersey, purchased the Ferris-Haggarty mine, with Willis George Emerson becoming a stockholder. The *Herald* reported that the company, with paid-up capital of twenty million dollars acquired ownership not only of the mine but also of the Grand Encampment smelter, the city water works, the Copper State Bank, the aerial tramway, a converter to be installed and a concentrator being erected, and the Emerson Electric Lighting Company. The WPA biography stated that the North American Copper Company was financed by "members of the Standard Oil crowd in Pennsylvania."

The tramway began operations in June 1903 amidst a huge celebration in Encampment, reported by the *Herald* as "the greatest event in the history of the State of Wyoming." As the first ore bucket passed Freeman Avenue, crowds of people downtown watched in amazement.

Emerson spoke at the event and the *Herald* carried this quotation from his speech: "It is not improbable to believe that in future years the ninth day of June will be held most sacred as a Memorial Day by the people of Encampment, Wyoming."

Emerson's promotional efforts worked quite well for him as well as for Encampment. By the early 1900s, his company had offices in Denver, Boston, and New York, as well as Encampment. Anderson's manuscript reported that Governor DeForest Richards appointed

W.G. Emerson. (Courtesy Wyoming Division of Cultural Resources)

Emerson as a commissioner to the Paris Exposition in 1900. Emerson served as vice chairman of the speakers' bureau for the Republican National Committee's 1900 campaign, and his speech, written in reply to Coin Harvey's "financial school" was issued as a Republican campaign document in 1900.

In 1900, the *Herald* reported yet another wonder—"a monster one-hundred-ton smelter." Emerson underwrote treasury stock to guarantee one hundred thousand dollars used to construct a pipeline and purchase machinery to complete a smelter with a capacity of one hundred tons daily.

He donated funds in 1902 to provide a bed in Encampment's Good Shepherd Hospital for patients who could not afford care.

Nichols wrote in "I Remember" that Emerson's name had been mentioned as a possible vice presidential candidate in the press. His novel, *Buell Hampton*, had also recently been published and received good reviews.

The Willis George Emerson Cornet Band organized and played for the July 4, 1902, celebration. Band members dressed as miners for the event.

In 1903, construction of the E&H Building began at the southwest corner of Freeman Avenue and Sixth Street. The building, erected by Emerson and W.C. Henry, covered two city lots and cost an estimated thirty-five thousand dollars, according to the *Herald*. Bricks were made by A.J. Rosander's brickyard near Encampment.

According to Candy Moulton's 1987 *Rawlins Daily Times* article, when the building was completed on August 12, 1904, it housed several businesses including the Copper State Bank, a barber shop, shoe-shine stand and laundry, a saloon, and offices of the North American Copper Company. Attorney Aaron Myers and Dr. Emmett Perdue also had offices in the building.

Emerson served as Wyoming's representative to the 1904 Saint Louis Exposition.

T.A. Larson in his *History of Wyoming* wrote of Emerson's plans to form a syndicate to build a new capital city in central Wyoming, midway between Casper, Rawlins, and Lander. "It was to be named Emerson, or some said Muskrat."

However, before the capital city issue could come to a vote, Emerson's future changed. The mining company's east coast 'system' sought a reorganization that did not include Emerson. The WPA biography summarized, "the 'system' proceeded to freeze out all the stockholders including Mr. Emerson. The 'system' then organized the Penn-Wyoming Copper Company and much litigation followed."

Emerson left the state before the November 1904 election when Cheyenne was selected as the state capital. The investigation and litigation concerning the copper company's financial reorganization continued. However, Anderson concluded in the biography that Emerson "emerged from the investigations untainted and clean as a 'hound's tooth.'"

Emerson's former banking partner, A.H. Heber, invited him to California in 1905 to "help colonize the Imperial Valley." He helped build the towns of Brawley, Imperial, Heber, and Calexico, California.

By 1906, the *Grand Encampment Herald* reported that the copper output from Wyoming might relieve a threatened copper shortage. The article carried an excerpt from the *London Financial News.*

As thrilling as it was, as stimulating to the economy, and as hopeful as the prospects were, the copper boom was not destined to last, not even with the industry's skilled promotions.

Velma Linford wrote in *Wyoming, Frontier State* that Emerson, "a glamorous promoter and author" purchased the Ferris-Haggarty for about a half million dollars and sold from twenty to thirty million dollars worth of stock. "This over-capitalization of the mine later resulted in the collapse of the stock value." In 1908, the company was indicted for over-capitalization and fraudulent stock sales.

Emerson managed to get his money out of the area before the dreadful crash wiped out the copper boom. Other investors were not that lucky.

Carl Ashley, an early-day Encampment resident, said in an April 1964 article in the *Saratoga Sun*, "I never could put the blame on Willis George for the big crash that came in 1908. Willis was a very well-educated man with a vision. Perhaps a dreamer who made his dreams come true, a very smooth talker, to sum it up a regular promoter and salesman; always had time to talk with a friend."

🌿🌿🌿

Emerson had married Bonnie O'Neal on June 4, 1907. He had two sons by a former marriage—Wilber Osgood Emerson and Fred Lee Emerson.

The *Denver Post* of December 21, 1918, reported that Emerson's enterprises had "made the name of Grand Encampment nationally famous and in the exploitation of which millions of dollars of real money changed hands." The newspaper stated that eventually all the assets of the several "interlocking enterprises" that Emerson had acquired with his associates were foreclosed on, earning about $150,000. None of the monies gained from the foreclosure was paid to stockholders.

Emerson went from Encampment to establish the Emerson Motors Company in Los Angeles. He became a life member of the Los Angeles Athletic Club and was also a member in several fraternal organizations. He died in Los Angeles, California in December 1918.

Carl Ashley stated, "Willis George and his associates were referred to as a bunch of swindlers and crooks by the people who were taken in by sales of stock, town lots, etc., but at the time Willis George sold out here the smelter was in operation, [and he left the] tramway running, the hills full of miners and a prosperous town and valley."

Alkali Ike Bellows

MERELY MENTIONING THE name "Alkali Ike" to those living now in the Saratoga and Encampment area inspires wry smiles and comments like, "He's a good one!" and "What a character!" Ike's exploits made him famous in the region, but little can be verified about the man. Reports of his death—and possibly reports about his life—were greatly exaggerated. Undoubtedly the legends surrounding the moniker befit Carbon County's rough-and-tumble past.

The Wyoming State Archives houses a biographical file on Ike, but confusion cloaks many of the details that could provide insight into his life. The file indicates that the nickname "Alkali Ike" was most likely attached to several men. Which one was really whom remains a mystery. Though it does not contain a birthdate, the file mentions Independence, Missouri, as a birthplace. Ike—or at least one of them—was apparently a Mason and a soldier who fought for the Confederacy during the Civil War.

The Alkali Ike best-known in Carbon County was a man named Daniel Bellows (or Bellews). He lived during the early 1900s, perhaps surviving into the mid-1950s and perhaps beyond. But his survival was questioned at least once, and probably many times.

The *Grand Encampment Herald* on May 20, 1904, carried the report of his death. The obituary was reprinted in its entirety in the following issue of the *Saratoga Sun*. Ike's colorful rebuttal appeared in the June 3, 1904, edition of the *Herald*, but the retraction never appeared in the *Sun*.

The erroneous obituary stated that humorist Bill Nye had made Alkali Ike "world renowned...as a typical western character." The reference was probably to a book called *Forty Liars and Other Lies*. With a title like that, whatever brought Ike to prominence could certainly have been just a big windy. And from a distance of nearly a century, which tale in the book revolves around Alkali Ike is unclear. The *Herald* reported Ike died at Fort Steele, stating, "Alkali Ike was the real thing without exaggeration. He was fated. He died with his boots on."

Some people remember Ike as a freighter, some as a miner, and some say that he worked as a ranch hand. He could have been all these and more. The October 26, 1898, issue of the *Denver Post* carried a story of a horrendous stage accident, with Alkali Ike mentioned as one of the guides on horseback. James Rankin, who had formerly served as Carbon County's sheriff, was the other.

The report stated that the Encampment-Rawlins stage, pulled by a six-horse team and driven by Charles "South Paw" Cumming, upset on a curve three miles from the "new mining town of Grand Encampment." South Paw, considered "the most expert stage driver in the West," had driven for Buffalo Bill's Wild West Show in the early 1880s.

Eighteen passengers, most from Colorado Springs and Cripple Creek, Colorado, were aboard the ill-fated stage. Of those, only three—W. G. Emerson, Clarence Edsall, and J. P. Wight—were uninjured. Those three jumped from the top of the stage as they saw what was coming. Other passengers and South Paw weren't so lucky. Two passengers and the driver were not expected to recover, having suffered severe head and spinal injuries in addition to broken bones. One passenger, Joseph Rankin, the man who had gained fame in 1879 as the heroic rider taking news of the Thornburgh battle from the White River Agency to Rawlins, suffered only slight internal injuries. Joseph Rankin's record run and heroism may have inspired his brother, James. The *Post* reported that James, "as soon as the wounded had been extricated from the stage, and stretched out upon the grass, put spurs to his horse and galloped to the Town company's office, and within half an hour fully a hundred people, with hastily improvised ambulance wagons, were on the scene of the tragedy and caring for the wounded."

The accident occurred during what was supposed to have been a pleasant exhibition of South Paw's driving expertise. The report stated, "Wreathing his long whip about the stage, he sent its buck-skin tassel at the flanks of the foremost horses, with a report that rang out like a pistol shot. The horses lunged forward into a terrific gallop, and again the swarthy dweller of the mountains and plains twirled his whip above him, and again the pistol like report reverberated over the valley and plains, reechoing from the precipitous mountains to the south and west. The maddened horses stretched away as if they were pursued by a band of blood thirsty Utes, and, indeed, it might well have seemed that they were, for at the second crack of the whip 'Alkali Ike' sent out from his lungs the war whoop of the Apache, and the veteran 'South Paw' answered back with a dismal howl, akin to the Indian summons to battle."

The thrilling adventure soon grew terrifying. The stage, swaying from side to side and sometimes leaving the ground on the bends in the road, missed a sharp curve, and "...its frightened occupants jostled on the inside like pebbles in a rattle box, while a dozen men went spinning into the air as if from a dynamite explosion." South Paw, badly injured, held the lines as the horses raced forward with the stage upturned behind them. James Rankin "plunged his foaming horse to the front, and prevented further disaster by grappling the leaders by the bits."

Follow-up reports on the accident were sketchy, but apparently Alkali Ike was not among the injured nor among the heroic.

Lora Webb Nichols, in her manuscript "I Remember," called Ike "a hard rock miner of no mean ability and also a good teamster." She recalled him as being able to secure work "whenever he really wanted a job. After weeks, or maybe months, of trying to 'drink the town dry,' he would go out on some job far from town and there he would stay, doing good and faithful work for his employer until the unquenchable thirst finally drew him back to town to complete the cycle once more." Nichols was somewhat fearful of Ike because of his drinking.

Historian Elva Evans, who compiles the column "Reflections from Our Files 100 Years Ago" for the *Saratoga Sun*, said former Saratoga resident Margaret Pearson, now-deceased, remembered Ike walking along beside the freight trains through the alkali flats. That was how Pearson thought Ike earned his nickname. Pearson recalled

he was always dirty and drunk. Pearson came to the area in 1906 and her family lived on Cow Creek near the freight line.

The *Herald* obituary took a different tack, stating that Nye named the man Alkali, using the term as slang for the word "alcohol." The paper also said that the nickname "Calamity Ike" might have suited him better. Stating his real name as Daniel Bellows, the paper reported he was accident-prone. "It was a black eye, or a wounded foot, or a broken jaw, or something, anything; and it was all the time. Reports from Fort Steele, where he expired, state that Ike broke his jaw again and quit the earth."

Saratoga resident and former mayor and publisher of the *Saratoga Sun*, R. Richard Perue, reproduced a historical photograph of the man known as Alkali Ike, which may give credence to the freighter theory or may indicate he was a miner or a tie hack. The photo shows Ike in a bar, probably the White Dog Saloon, in the mountain mining town of Dillon in 1902. Pistol in one hand and

"Alkali Ike," holding pistol and knife in the White Dog Saloon. (Photo courtesy Historical Reproductions by Dick Perue, Grand Encampment Museum.)

knife in the other, Ike's eyes are rolled back in his head as if he's about to pass out. All the eyes of the others in the bar, however, even those of a young woman depicted in a poster, are—with good reason—focused intently on Ike.

Perue is uncertain if the photograph was taken by Lora Webb Nichols or by Jack Ledbetter, but Nichols would have been just a teenager at the time, so it was unlikely that she would have been photographing events in a bar. Perue said that Nichols rarely took bar photos.

A July Fourth memory recorded in the July 17, 1903, *Herald* tells of the celebration in the local tie camp, mentioning "Red Nose Ike." It is entirely possible, given Alkali Ike's reputation for indulging in liquor, that this new nickname was yet another pseudonym for

Alkali. The newspaper reported the celebration was a dandy. Near the Jessie mine several explosions were set off in honor of the event. In the tie camp, "each state in the union was saluted by the explosion of one stick of giant powder with a bunch of fire crackers added for the recently acquired Spanish colonies." Local bars called Robbers' Roost and Hackers Delight employed a double staff of bartenders, but "nothing of an exciting nature occurred except a couple of cutting affairs followed by a duel with shotguns between two noted desperadoes named Missouri Jack and Red Nose Ike."

Somehow, a poker chip got stuck in Missouri Jack's gun muzzle and split the charge. The report stated that Red Nose Ike lost both ears and Missouri Jack "received the full charge from Ike's gun. Missouri was immediately dropped into an old prospect hole and...a lynching bee was formed with Ike as the central figure, hanging him from the limb of a pine." Apparently this was all in fun, because a dance followed the lynching and "lasted until midnight, when all returned to their homes with patriotism and enthusiasm."

However, if this surreal account is to be taken at face value, this Red Nose Ike must not have been the same Ike mentioned earlier because records kept at the Grand Encampment Museum indicate Lora Webb Nichols interviewed Ike in 1954. That recorded interview could not be located.

Yet another account, a poem written by the late Maude Wenonah Willford and included in her 1963 book, *Over the Hills and Prairies of Wyoming*, gives Ike a slightly more respectable air. Depicting him as a ranch hand, Willford pokes fun at Ike's luck with the ladies. Her poem reads:

> This is Alkali Ike I'm tellin' about.
> He works for the A—A.
> In summer he hazes little doggies about
> In winter he forks out their hay.
>
> In color, Ike's hair is a strawberry roan,
> His face is as freckled as sin.
> He's long, and lank, and limber, and lean,
> With a devilish cleft in his chin.

In straddlin' a bronc or twirlin' a rope
Was he good, Pard? I'm tellin' a man!
If he couldn't scratch both head and the tail
There's nary a puncher who can.

Now this Alkali Ike was a keen judge of stock
As ever rode out on the range
He could squint at a steer, guess at his weight
And hand back a nickel in change.

At spottin' a horse or selectin' a bull
He was good as ever you'll find;
But when it came to pickin' a girl
The poor fool! He must have gone blind!

Ike married a gal named Sally O'Moore
She came up from Medicine Bow
She was shy as a colt, just ready to bolt
All cinched up and ready to go.

She was balky and stubborn with a wild roving eye
To lead she just could not be broke
She was skittish and snorty and tricky and mean
A rearin' right back on the rope!

Poor Ike! He got stung like a bee on the nose,
His range knowledge betrayed him somehow,
For it was Ike, himself, who got halterbroke
And hitched right up to the plow!

A search of cemetery indices in the Saratoga and Encampment area, including the defunct town of Dillon, revealed no evidence of Ike. Perhaps Alkali Ike traveled to another area of the country and met his real demise elsewhere.

His premature obituary—oddly enough the first document often mentioned with complete confidence in its accuracy whenever his name comes up—stated that during the final years of his life, Ike was "principally engaged...in the cause of temperance, having taken a personal responsibility in putting down liquor." That's one fact most descriptions of Alkali Ike are in agreement about.

Ike's rebuttal to the false account of his death provides insight into his character. The June 3, 1904, *Herald* carried the story. In a special report from Fort Steele, the newspaper reported, "'Alkali Ike' respectfully declines to accept the report as true that he is dead. He says that it is a ——— lie, and that he will outlive the !?!?!?!? who started the report."

The newspaper reported, "Although the statement has been printed around the world that Alkali Ike is dead, he is indeed as lively as ever, and it isn't his spirit that is here either, although he is often quite close to the spirit realm."

A body had been discovered near Fort Steele about a month prior to the report of Ike's death. Since Ike had not been seen around the area for awhile, people jumped to the wrong conclusion and buried the badly decomposing body, certain that it was Ike. "So the boys killed him off, as they have done before two or three times, and the newspapers gave Ike another series of obituaries," the paper stated.

After this particular falsehood, Ike invited "every man who believes that [I am] a dead one to come to Fort Steele with spending money." The losers were to buy Ike the best drinks available, and he promised "to stay sober notwithstanding."

Certainly colorful and immediately recognizable through legend, Alkali Ike remains an enigma. The *Herald* obituary reported, "Ike left no autobiography by which a synopsis of his life could be obtained but he has been known to talk occasionally when in the mood and he has told some great tales on himself." Ironically, it further stated, "The memory of this odd character will fade with the frontier history of Wyoming."

But Alkali Ike and the tales surrounding his life and death did not fade. His legend, like many tales surrounding frontier history, survives.

Ed Haggarty & George Ferris

ENTREPRENEURS OFTEN TAKE RISKS to achieve success. The same principle applies to miners. The hope of striking it rich overshadows the months, sometimes years, of toil and investment necessary. There are no guarantees with such risks.

Ed Haggarty took a risk with mining, and it paid off handsomely. The oft-told story is that Haggarty was a sheepherder who stumbled across rich veins of ore while working for George Ferris. However, Haggarty's own account, told to Agnes Spring Wright in the 1930s, claims he was not herding sheep at all, but was a skilled and savvy prospector, searching for what he found.

Haggarty came to Wyoming from Cumberland, England, where he was born in the 1860s. He tried prospecting because he hadn't been able to save money while working for wages, according to notes taken by Wyoming historian Charles G. Coutant and printed in the booklet, *The Grand Encampment*. Haggarty did his first mining work in 1894 in Cripple Creek, Colorado, but he first prospected around Sandstone, an area about ten miles from the Rudefeha—his lucky strike.

Haggarty spent what money he had doing assessment work on the several claims he'd taken, Coutant said.

In July 1897, Haggarty made a discovery near Battle Lake. The area was rich in red, spongy iron ore. According to an article in the *Rawlins Daily Times* in 1976 written by Peter Bielak, "Haggarty had been told earlier by a miner from Douglas Mountain Mining Company that the ore was a sure indication of copper." Haggarty saw green stains, another indication that he'd discovered a copper vein.

The next month, Haggarty found the red copper oxide vein. Although the mineral deposits were not large enough to be considered profitable, Haggarty felt the possibilities of a paying mine were good. He convinced his partners, Robert Deal, J.M. Rumsey, and George Ferris—who had given Haggarty a grubstake—to allow him to continue to work the claim through the winter.

Rumsey sold his interest to Ferris for one thousand dollars, and Deal backed out, too. Haggarty and Ferris risked their savings on the claim. In August 1898, they drilled a thirty foot shaft and struck a rich vein of copper.

Production at the mine increased dramatically. In 1899, Haggarty sold his interest to Ferris for thirty thousand dollars. Little did he know that only three years later, in 1902, the North American Copper Company would purchase the mine for the sum of one million dollars.

After selling his interest, Haggarty returned to his native England. He wrote a letter to his former partner, Robert Deal, saying that when he arrived there he found his parents renting a farm. Haggarty paid their debts and purchased a cottage for them in town. He made certain they were financially secure until they died, and his brother took charge of the farm.

The *Saratoga Sun* carried an article about Ed Haggarty in March 1899. The paper reported, "Nearly everyone has heard of Ed Haggarty, the man who discovered the now famous copper mine, the Rudefeha, but perhaps few have made his acquaintance, for he is a quiet, soft spoken man, not given to pushing himself forward."

He apparently was also kind-hearted, as he built a schoolhouse in 1899 in the mining town of Battle. The building was also used as a church.

The *Sun* said of Haggarty, "He says that he has never found a place in all his wanderings that suited him so well as where he was so very prosperous."

Haggarty sold his mining interests too early to make a fortune, but the money he made allowed him to care for his family and enjoy life.

In October 1937, the *Sun* reported Haggarty had suffered a slight stroke, saying, "Encampment probably owes more for its existence today [to Haggarty] than any other one man who actually aided in its development."

🪶🪶🪶

Haggarty's early employer, George Ferris, also prospered from the copper mine, but his enjoyment of the fortune proved short-lived.

A manuscript by Fay Anderson, prepared for the Works Project Administration, reported Ferris was born in Michigan and served in Company D of the Seventh Michigan Calvary during the Civil War. After four years and promotions for meritorious conduct, he mustered out with the rank of lieutenant and returned to Michigan.

After a one-year stay in his home state, Ferris came to Carbon County, searching for employment and prospecting, too. Ferris ranched with Joe Hurt on a Platte River ranch located about twelve miles from Fort Steele. In 1889, he sold out his interest in the cattle and began raising sheep.

Jane Provorse wrote in "The Ferris Mansion" in the October 2, 1983, issue of *Wyoming Horizons* that Ferris came to Wyoming to hunt buffalo for the Wells-Fargo Stage Company. The stage company furnished meat to crews working on the Union Pacific Railroad and later invested in the cattle and sheep industries.

Anderson wrote of Ferris, "...During his lifetime [he was considered] one of the best known citizens of Carbon County, Wyoming, and one of the most honorable and enterprising cattlemen of the Platte River Valley." She gave Ferris "the credit of the stability of the mining industry, as it exists in Carbon County today."

Ferris also showed an active interest in politics. The Republican represented the state at the constitutional convention held when Wyoming Territory earned statehood, and he served two terms in the Wyoming Legislature. He also served as a county commissioner. The *Cheyenne Daily Leader* dubbed Ferris "The Copper King of Wyoming" in August 1900.

Ferris, by that time, owned the controlling interest in the mine, having bought both Rumsey's and Haggarty's shares. The newspaper reported that he employed 250 men and four hundred horses, making average daily shipments of eighty thousand pounds of ore to the Denver smelter. Expenses were thirty thousand dollars each month, but Ferris felt that it was "the beginning."

"Mr. Ferris has been the life and soul of the enterprises, staking everything and crowding development to the greatest possible extent.

This was the explanation given by Mr. I. C. Miller of the vast amount of work that had been done in so short a period," the newspaper reported.

At that time, buildings were being erected to prepare for winter, including boarding houses and dwellings. The newspaper reported that the company was building a small town for its own use, cutting 2,500 cords of pine and hauling hay and grain and other supplies in large quantities.

In 1899, Ferris and his wife, Julia, began building a large home in Rawlins so they would have ample space for their seven children. Today it is known as the "Ferris Mansion."

George Ferris's activities soon ended, however. He was traveling home from the mine, driving his carriage. At Snow Slide Hill, his team caught the scent of a team of horses killed a year earlier in an avalanche and became frightened and unmanageable. Ferris was thrown from the carriage and killed.

Julia finished the mansion, a three-story, twenty-one room, Victorian house, in 1903. She lived there until her death in 1931. The Ferris Mansion was listed on the National Register of Historic Places in the 1980s. More recent residents noticed a "ghostly presence" there, according to Provorse. They think that it may be Cecil, George and Julia's son, who died when he accidentally shot himself with a pistol in 1904.

M.D. Houghton

THE OLD ADAGE, "the pen is mightier than the sword" was meant to apply to the written word, but it could easily be applied to a little-known Wyoming artist of the early twentieth century.

Merritt Dana Houghton drew pencil sketches of many Wyoming sites in the late 1800s and early 1900s. He provided a unique historical record of mining areas, forts, and ranches. After finishing his pencil sketches, he traced them with pen to create the views for which he earned recognition.

Houghton sketched as if he flew above his subjects, using a wide-angle to encompass as much detail as possible.

His Wyoming life began in 1875, when he came to Laramie. Not much is known of his early years, but he was born in Otsego, Michigan, on May 31, 1846, one of nine children. His father was from New York and his mother from Canada.

In Laramie, Houghton worked as a school teacher and also as a photographer.

Ida Purdy Harrell recounted her memories of the artist and his wife, Frances, for the Works Projects Administration Writers' Project. Harrell met them in the 1890s, when Houghton taught school at Cummings City, which later became known as Jelm.

"They were very devoted to each other and much alike," Harrell wrote. "Both were well-educated, had high ideals, and [were] the best friends and neighbors one could wish for."

Harrell stated that Houghton was a good teacher who set a good example for youngsters. "He did not drink or use tobacco, and no one ever heard him use bad language," she wrote.

Houghton also had another talent—that of creating dress patterns. According to Harrell, he could look at a picture and create a pattern with a perfect fit.

The Houghtons moved to Carbon and Rawlins in the years after 1875.

An advertisement in the November 8, 1879, issue of the *Carbon County Journal* announced that the "photographic rooms at Houghton's" would do "all kinds of photographic work." Along with photographs and picture enlargements, fermotypes and views were included in the "satisfaction guaranteed" services available.

Candy Moulton wrote in the article "Ranch Artist," published in *Wyoming Horizons,* that in 1880 Houghton, who was the County Superintendent for the Rawlins schools at the time, found himself embroiled in controversy. The school board rehired teacher H. F. Belcher, but Houghton would not give him a certificate. The school board won, allowing Belcher to finish the school year. When Houghton's term expired, he wasn't even nominated for re-election.

The Houghtons moved to Buffalo, located in the north-eastern part of Wyoming, in 1884. In Buffalo, he advertised his photographic studio, but the venture wasn't very successful. It was hard to make a living as a photographer in those days.

Around 1890, the Houghtons were again located in Laramie. Frances Houghton had developed cataracts on both eyes. Houghton sold his equipment and studio to pay for her surgeries. He again taught school.

But his artistic talents continued to emerge. He began to create sketches of local ranches. He often rode from ranch to ranch, teaching school and always drawing. His drawings were often created while he sat on a hill, giving the sketches the feeling of being seen from above with a wide perspective.

For nine years, Houghton worked both at teaching and at his sketches, which proved popular items. Then, in 1899, C. G. Coutant asked him to illustrate his book, *History of Wyoming.* Houghton sketched sites along the Overland Trail, including stage stations. He also created views of Forts Bridger, Laramie, Fetterman, and Reno.

Coutant wrote that Houghton's work was historically accurate because he didn't just draw as he thought it might look, but the artist

M.D. Houghton. (Courtesy Wyoming Division of Cultural Resources)

took the time to discuss the subjects with local pioneers who remembered the sites.

According to an article written by Michael Amundson and published in the Autumn 1994 issue of *Montana: The Magazine of Western History,* Houghton worked on other sketches as he traveled through Wyoming, producing two dozen pictures during the summer of 1899. Some of these pictures, which include ranches and towns located on the Oregon Trail, were done in watercolors. Houghton also sketched the town of Fort Collins, Colorado—his first large-scale view of a town, with the Rockies rising in the background.

After nine years of hard work, Houghton's creativity began to pay off. Amundson reported that the 1901 Industrial Edition of the *Laramie Republican* published several of his ranch drawings, and the *Wyoming Press* of Evanston published the drawings the next year.

The next few years were prolific ones for Houghton. During the years 1902–1904, Houghton created nearly one hundred sketches and compiled two books of illustrations. He also sold photo-engraved prints. A 1903 view of Saratoga and a topographical map of Encampment's mining district in the same year are used to make reproductions today.

Houghton spent part of the summer of 1902 in Encampment, visiting the mining camps and sketching the area. The *Grand Encampment Herald* printed reproductions of several of his works in 1902 and 1903.

The April 9, 1903, *Saratoga Sun* reported Houghton's completion of "a very fine picture of the ranch of N.K. Boswell on the Big Laramie river in Albany County." The picture was five feet long, and "one that should commend Mr. Houghton's work as that of an artist."

Houghton's book, entitled *A Portfolio of Wyoming Views: The Platte Valley and the Grand Encampment Mining District*, was published by the *Herald* in early 1904.

Included in the book are views of now abandoned mining towns, including Dillon, Battle, Rambler, and Rudefeha. A Saratoga view is included, along with some ranch views, the tramway station, and the Copper Giant mine.

The book sold for one dollar per copy. Lora Webb Nichols wrote in her manuscript, "I Remember", that Houghton's book "enjoyed a fine sale," but noted that at the time of her writing in the 1950s it had already "become very rare."

Perhaps one of Houghton's best-known sketches is a 1904 view of Grand Encampment, including the copper smelting works and its aerial tramway. The tramway, heralded as an engineering wonder, earned international recognition as the longest aerial tramway in the world.

Houghton's second volume, published in 1904, was titled *Views of Southern Wyoming: 1904 Copper Belt Edition*. Along with previously published views, the book included a drawing of the Fort Steele tie loading plant of the Carbon Timber Company, the Ferris-Haggarty mine, and the town of Grand Encampment.

Vera Oldman, past president of the Grand Encampment Museum, estimates that around seventy of Houghton's originals are still in circulation. Ranchers and their families still cherish sketches created by the artist, many of which remain in their homes. Encampment resident Viola Bixler owns a rare colored Houghton drawing of her grandfather Kels Nickell's Iron Mountain ranch. (Nickell was the father of Willie Nickell who was allegedly murdered by legendary hired-gun Tom Horn.) The Wyoming State Museum in Cheyenne houses a large collection of Houghton's work. Other Wyoming collections of Houghton drawings are kept at the American Heritage Center, University of Wyoming in Laramie, the Carbon County Museum in Rawlins, and the Grand Encampment Museum in Encampment.

Other Wyoming sites that Houghton sketched include Big Horn City, Dayton, Dietz, Monarch, and Sheridan. Although Houghton's views often depict Wyoming sites, the artist also created sketches in Washington.

Houghton and his wife moved to Hillyard, Washington, around 1906 to be near his brother and in an effort to improve Frances's health. He drew Mullan, Idaho, a small mining town, on his way, according to Amundson. While living in Hillyard, a Spokane suburb, Houghton created sketches of Five Mile Prairie and Green Acres, small nearby communities. He also created a topographical view of the Empire Coal and Coke Company holdings in the eastern portion of the state.

In 1914, Houghton created a bird's-eye view of Sunset Farms of West Spokane, a sketch Amundson believes to be his last. Further details of the Houghtons' lives in Washington are sparse.

Both Houghton and his wife succumbed to the flu epidemic in 1919. They died within sixteen hours of each other. He was seventy-three-years old.

Houghton's works have recently sparked renewed interest in the Carbon County area. In 1994, Amundson, who also works as visiting instructor of history at Idaho State University, presented a program on Houghton at the Grand Encampment Museum's opening day. R. Richard Perue, a Saratoga photographer specializing in reproduction work, is compiling reproductions of Houghton's books.

Amundson wrote in his article, "When viewed collectively, Houghton's portfolio presents a firsthand account of the western landscape.... Further, the fact that few of Houghton's subjects grew into big cities or vast ranches, testifies to his depiction of the lives of common people."

Velma Linford, in *Wyoming, Frontier State*, wrote, "Wyoming's industrial progress as well as valuable historical data is preserved in the pen-and-ink and charcoal drawings of Merritt Dana Houghton."

Without the mighty pen of M.D. Houghton, many historical details of Wyoming might have been lost forever. But through the artist's unique perspective, ranches and mines and forts have been preserved for more generations to view.

Charles E. Winter

THE MAN TRAVELING ON A Pennsylvania train in 1903 gazed out the window at the sites of the Lehigh Valley. As the wheels clacked their monotonous rhythm, the man thought of his home, a thousand miles away.

He missed his family. He missed his home.

The young attorney took a memorandum book from his vest pocket and began writing.

> "In the far and mighty west
> Where the crimson sun seeks rest,
> There's a growing splendid State that lies above....
> On the breast of this great land,
> Where the massive Rockies stand,
> There's Wyoming, young and strong, the State I love...."

The words poured from the young man's heart. He wrote five verses and a chorus about his state, Wyoming. When he arrived in Grand Encampment, he typed his creation and placed it in his desk.

Several months passed before Charles E. Winter presented those words to Earle Clemens, another Encampment resident. Clemens had been editor of the *Grand Encampment Herald* for several years. Winter asked Clemens, who was also a talented musician, to set the words to music.

Clemens, too, placed the words in his desk. When he again ran across them, he took up pen and ink and wrote a solo verse and a quartet chorus.

At about this same time, both Clemens and Winter attended the State Industrial Convention in Sheridan as delegates. They, along with a couple of men from Sheridan, formed an impromptu quartet and sang the new musical creation. People attending the convention liked it so much that they declared it the new state song.

The song gained national fame soon after that. It was played on Wyoming Day at the St. Louis World's Fair in 1904, at the World's Fair in Portland, Oregon, in 1905, and at the Panama Exposition in San Francisco in 1915.

In the 1930s, Charles Winter heard it played yet again—this time by the United States Marine Band in Washington, D. C., and in Puerto Rico, in march tempo.

Other words flowed from the pen of Charles Winter. He wrote *Grandon of the Sierra*, his first novel, in 1907. In 1913, he wrote *Ben Warman*, a novel which a Colorado film company later made into a movie called *The Vanishing Strain*.

In 1932, Winter wrote *Four Hundred Million Acres*, a study of public lands and resources and state and federal conservation. The book, said to be the first of its kind ever published, was used as a textbook in several western universities.

Winter's last novel, *Gold of Freedom*, was written while he served as Attorney General in Puerto Rico in the 1930s. The story was set in the mining area of South Pass, Wyoming, but it was written on the rooftop of a 450-year-old palace in Puerto Rico.

In the foreword, Winter wrote, "The gold of freedom transcends infinitely the gold and other products of the earth but they are complementary. Both are indispensable. *Gold of Freedom*, this story of one area, a cross-section of the west, is written in the hope that its history, its rugged characters, the heroism, deeds and progress of free people on the frontier of free land, may help to inspire the return to and preservation of the American dream."

Winter was born on September 13, 1870, in Muscatine, Iowa. He attended school in Iowa and Nebraska, earning a degree in philosophy from Nebraska Wesleyan University in 1892.

Winter's father and mother, William and Wilhelmine (Fiegenbaum) Winter, were natives of Germany who came to America with their parents and eventually settled in Missouri. After moving to Chicago, William became a circuit rider in the Illinois and Iowa

Methodist ministry. He died in 1881, at the age of fifty-six, while his son was still a youngster.

Charles Winter earned admittance to the Nebraska bar in 1895 and became clerk of the county court in Omaha, a position he retained for four years. While in Omaha, Winter married Augusta F. Hutchinson in 1896. The couple had three sons—Stanley, Warren, and Franklin.

Winter went into private legal practice in 1900 and moved to Encampment in 1902, where he joined Spencer E. Phelps as a partner in the firm of Phelps and Winter. The two men had been college friends.

Lora Webb Nichols, in her manuscript, "I Remember," recalled the 1902 Fourth of July celebration in Encampment as a "very good one. Attorney Charles E. Winter, 'The Silver-Tongued Orator,' gave the address of the day."

Nichols also recalled an incident reported in the January 23, 1904, issue of the *Grand Encampment Herald*. Winter and William Matthews had attempted to travel in the mountains near the town of Battle to do some contract work on a property owned by the Standard Copper Mining Company.

The two men got caught in a blizzard. After surviving without food or water for twenty-two hours, they managed to find the town of Rambler.

The newspaper reported, "Winter came out of the ordeal with his toes slightly tinged by the frost and Matthews had the tips of his ears frosted. Both came out of the death trap with sufficient experience with mountains and midwinter weather to hold them for awhile."

While living in Encampment, Winter won election to a three-year term on the school board.

Winter had been interested in politics since college, where he'd been active in the Republican party. In 1912, he ran as a candidate for the position of Congressional representative on the Progressive ticket. This campaign laid the foundation for future, successful Congressional campaigns.

The Winter family moved to Casper in 1913, and Augusta died there that year, leaving Winter with three young sons. About that same time the Wyoming's legislature created a new judicial district.

Charles E. Winter. (Courtesy Wyoming Division of Cultural Resources)

Governor Joseph M. Carey appointed Winter as judge of the Sixth Judicial District. Winter was then elected to serve a six-year term as judge in 1914.

In 1915, Winter married Alice R. Maltby of Spokane, Washington. Before the completion of his term as judge, he resigned to return to the private practice of law.

Winter served as chairman of several Liberty Bond loan campaigns during World War I and was appointed to the judge advocate's department in December 1918. His rank would have been Major, but Winter declined the appointment because the war had ended.

But the political arena drew him again. In 1922, he won his first election to Congress as a Republican. In 1924 and 1926, he won the seat again by even larger majorities. The voters clearly liked and respected Representative Charles E. Winter.

His reputation as a silver-tongued orator continued to grow. In addition to a 1925 New York radio broadcast of one of his speeches, Winter delivered speeches in all forty-eight states during his career and often addressed organizations interested in protection and development of western resources.

The *Casper Tribune-Herald* reported in 1948 after Winter's death, that he was "a literary stylist of exceptional attainments." The newspaper called him "a fluent and easy speaker" who organized his material well and was "supported by an unusually retentive memory."

In April 1925, the radio station WMCA in New York carried Winter's address about Wyoming. The *Casper Herald* of April 25 called the speech "a eulogy of the marvels of Wyoming and the west." The newspaper estimated that "hundreds of thousands" of people had listened to Winter.

Winter explained that the Equality state's slogan at the time was "stop roaming—try Wyoming." The speech also contained many facts about Wyoming, including its firsts in allowing women the right to vote and the election of a woman governor, Nellie Tayloe Ross.

Winter said, "Wyoming is the greatest undeveloped state in the Union...she has unlimited opportunities and bestows limitless ambitions; she has immeasurable potentialities and she will bestow on all who seek her, with faith and with work, hope, power, mastery and success."

The October 1, 1926, issue of the *Inland Oil Index* reported that Winter gave "one of the most scholarly and brilliant addresses" at the joint Denver convention of the American Mining Congress, American Institute of Mining and Metallurgical Engineers, American Association of Petroleum Geologists, and American Silver Producers Association. The publication carried his speech in its entirety.

This speech focused on public lands. Winter believed that what was best for states containing large amounts of public lands was ultimately best for the nation. At the time of his address, 184 million acres of unreserved and unappropriated public lands remained, with the bulk of that acreage in the eleven western states. About 180 million acres had already been reserved by the government for use as Indian reservations, national parks, power sites, and forest reserves.

Winter said, "The International treaties and the ordinances of 1887 expressly provide and the constitution requires that the area acquired under the treaties with Great Britain, Spain, France, and Mexico, shall be formed into free independent states 'upon an equal footing with the original 13 states.' The 11 public land states have not been upon an equal footing such as was expressly provided for; we are not now on an equal footing with the original states or any of the other states and if Government Federal control is to continue indefinitely and increase instead of diminish, we never can, or will be, upon that parity or equality with the original states of the Union." Winter called this a violation of the country's policy that had been in force for a century.

His recommendations included decreasing rather than raising fees for public land use and promoting the right of free range, which he felt would leave the land open for settlement. Winter said that the cattle industry was already bankrupt and couldn't afford to pay additional fees for grazing.

He closed by saying, "Let us complete the American system of local government over local things; stop centralization in Washington; eliminate bureau government; relieve the people generally of costly national machinery; perfect the sovereignty of the public land states, so that in deed and in truth we will be upon an equal footing with the 13 original and all the other states. We ask no more than they have had."

He asked only for "equality, equal dignity, and authority" for the public land states.

The *Guernsey Gazette* of February 19, 1926, reported that Winter hoped to gain preservation of Forts Laramie and Bridger as national monuments. The paper reported that Winter, "as author of the state song, is known as 'the Bard of Wyoming'...."

Winter also productively used his oratorical skill in Congress. In 1948 the *Casper Tribune-Herald* said that Representative Winter's first bill passed into law authorized the holding of federal court terms in Casper, Wyoming. This legislation resulted in increased appropriations for the federal building and post office in Casper. He also introduced a bill which conferred jurisdiction on the Court of Claims to hear the lawsuit of the Shoshone Indian tribe. The passage of the bill resulted in a more than four million dollar judgment.

Winter also worked to pass a bill which confirmed title of the western states to the school districts and included minerals. Five hundred contests brought by the Secretary of the Interior were dismissed as a result. Another bill introduced by Winter appropriated $200,000 for research on extraction of potash and alumina from surface deposits including the Leucite Hills in Sweetwater County. This bill also passed.

Winter supported legislation for the Railroad Labor Board estate, according to the *Casper Tribune-Herald*, "recognizing the right of labor to collective bargaining by representatives of its own choosing." Winter studied the railroad labor problem extensively and ultimately influenced the creation of the railroad retirement system.

He also helped pass a law which increased the size of isolated public land tracts available for purchase from 150 to 320 acres.

Winter served as a member of the reclamation committee which passed the Boulder Dam bill. That bill reserved to Wyoming, Utah, Colorado and New Mexico about seven-and-one-half-million acre feet of water from the Colorado River Basin.

He helped re-establish the appropriations for the Riverton reclamation project and the Deaver division of the Shoshone project after the Secretary of the Interior decided to abandon them.

In 1928, he sought the Senate nomination but was defeated in the general election by Senator John B. Kendrick. Winter campaigned again for the Senate and the House, and though he wasn't elected, he was considered a "formidable" candidate.

In 1930, he declined an appointment as Solicitor General of the Department of Agriculture to make a run for the Senate. After that unsuccessful bid, Winter earned another appointment.

President Herbert Hoover in 1932 appointed him as Attorney General of Puerto Rico, a position he held for nineteen months. When the Governor General of Puerto Rico had to be absent for a time, Winter temporarily filled that office.

In 1936, when President Roosevelt was elected, he asked for Winter's resignation. Winter did resign, although he felt that the appointment was to have been binding for the full term of his assignment.

The *Casper Tribune-Herald* stated, "[Winter's] interest in politics never abated, and he was a vigorous campaigner even in his later years."

He continued to practice law, and his son, Warren, joined him as a partner in his practice in Casper.

Winter was active in several organizations, including serving twice as a president of both the Natrona County and Wyoming State Bar Associations. He was a thirty-second degree Mason, a member of the Korein temple of the Shriners, and was a past master of the Encampment Lodge. He also belonged to other fraternal organizations.

Winter retained his interest in literature. He was an organizer of the Casper Literary Club. In addition, he was active in the Kiwanis, the pioneer society, the American Bar Association, and the United States Chamber of Commerce.

His second wife, Alice, assisted her husband with his campaigns, traveling with him, speaking on broadcasts and organizing Republican women. The *Casper Tribune-Herald* reported that she had been a charming hostess at events in Washington and Puerto Rico. She became the chairman of the volunteer service of the American Red Cross on the island after a hurricane. She also lectured on life in Puerto Rico throughout Wyoming in schools, churches, and at clubs.

Alice, a teacher and a nurse, had graduated from the National Republican School for Women in Washington, D. C., in 1923, and she attended George Washington University in the fall of 1924, majoring in journalism.

Each year that the Winters were in Washington, D. C., she hosted "Wyoming Day" for Wyoming students.

❦❦❦

The state song, *Wyoming,* was revised in 1920 by Professor George E. Knapp, a professor of voice at the University of Wyoming. The revision set the tempo to march time and lowered the voice range to facilitate popular singing. The new version, titled *Wyoming March Song,* retained Charles E. Winter's original lyrics. The final verse contains the words:

> "Mine it is, Wyoming's star
> Home it leads me, near or far.
> O Wyoming! All my heart and love you've won...."

Winter, who stayed steadfastly loyal to Wyoming even though he had come from the midwest, died in April 1948, at the age of seventy-seven. The residents of the state remained loyal to him, too.

The *Casper Tribune-Herald* stated, "His great integrity and fair dealing were widely recognized by his host of friends and acquaintances."

His wife, Alice, survived him until 1961.

Winter's words became a part of Wyoming's history. They continue today as a reminder of a young man who, while pining for his home on a trip to the east, recognized his abiding love for the state.

Acknowledgements

MANY PEOPLE ASSISTED me with research for this book, and I owe them an enormous debt of gratitude for their time and effort. The staff at the Wyoming State Archives (Department of Parks and Cultural Resources) in Cheyenne gave gracious help and encouragement whenever I needed it. Special thanks to Cindy Brown, Ann Nelson, Jean Brainerd, and LaVaughn Bresnahan at that office. Many of the newspaper articles and manuscripts I consulted came from the files at the archives, which hold a wealth of biographical information, photographs, and other resources.

The staff at the American Heritage Center, University of Wyoming, Laramie, also provided information and assistance, and special thanks to D. Claudia Thompson and Jennifer King, who assisted me in the reading room; Matt Sprinkle, audio/visual; and Rick Ewig, acting director. The AHC, too, houses many valuable historical records, including taped oral interviews, books, manuscripts, and letters, which help bring the past into clearer focus.

Local museum curators and organizations also helped bring many stories to light. For the assistance of Nancy Wallis and Kathy Lane, former directors, and Pat Bensen, director of the Saratoga Museum; the Saratoga Historical and Cultural Association; Jean Martinez, former curator, and Joyce Kelley, curator at the Carbon County Museum, Rawlins, Wyoming; and Dorthy Wolfard, Lillian Barnes, Vera Oldman, and others at the Grand Encampment Museum; I am deeply grateful. I could not have written this book without their help.

Candy Moulton continues to provide valuable support and encouragement. Dick Perue helped by reproducing historical photographs when necessary. Lindy Smith, Carbon County Clerk of District Court, also assisted with research. Librarians at both the Saratoga and Rawlins Branches of the Carbon County Library gave much needed assistance.

Jennifer Bosley, research historian at the Colorado Historical Society in Denver, Colorado; Kathey Swan at the Denver Public Library, Western History Department; and Elinor Mullens, historian at the Episcopal Diocese in Laramie, Wyoming, provided additional help.

Hats off to Dr. George Gill, University of Wyoming anthropology professor and forensic science/osteology specialist, and Kristi McMahan for sharing their research, and to Dr. Mark Miller who reviewed my manuscript and offered helpful suggestions for improvement. He also patiently responded to my request for updated information in the continuing research on Big Nose George.

My husband, Eugene, my sister-in-law, Cid, and their parents, Mr. and Mrs. E. W. Walck, Sr., gave me unlimited quantities of time and patience throughout this project and continue to encourage me in myriad ways.

My thanks to Teense Willford who gave permission to use his grandmother Maude Wenonah Willford's poem on Alkali Ike.

This acknowledgement would not be complete without also thanking Gladys Beery, who wrote *Sinners and Saints: Tales from Old Laramie City*, which provided the inspiration for this book, and Nancy Curtis, my publisher, for her kind, patient guidance and her skillful editing.

Bibliography

"A Sketch of Major Thornburgh," *Cheyenne Daily Leader*, 3 October 1879.

"A Son Returns and Makes Glad the Hearts of His Aged Parents," *Saratoga Sun,* March 1899.

Adams, Ramon F. *Six-Guns & Saddle Leather: A Bibliography of Books and Pamphlets on Western Outlaws and Gunmen.* Norman, Okla.: University of Oklahoma Press, 1954.

Aikman, Duncan. *Calamity Jane and the Lady Wildcats.* New York: Henry Holt & Company, 1927.

Alcorn, Gay Day. *Tough Country: The History of the Saratoga and Encampment Valley 1825-1895.* Saratoga, Wyo.: The Legacy Press, 1984.

———. "The Savage House." Presentation at the annual trek of the Saratoga Historical and Cultural Association, Saratoga, Wyo., August 1994.

———. "Saint Barnabas Episcopal Church of Saratoga Formerly the Church of Heavenly Rest," Manuscript, 1994.

"'Alkali Ike' is Dead," *Grand Encampment Herald*, 20 May 1904.

"'Alkali Ike' Not a Dead One," *Grand Encampment Herald*, 3 June 1904.

Amundson, Michael A. "Pen Sketches of Promise," *Montana, The Magazine of Western History,* Autumn 1994.

Anderson, Fay. "Hon. George Ferris,*"* MSS, Works Progress Administration (WPA) biographical file 311, Wyoming State Archives, 20 December 1940.

———. "Hon. W. L. Kuykendall," MSS, WPA biographical file 554, Wyoming State Archives, 31 December 1940.

———. "Willis George Emerson," MSS, WPA biographical file 1808, Wyoming State Archives, 1938.

———. "Frederick G. Wolf," MSS, WPA biographical file 1051, Wyoming State Archives, nd.

———. "Paris Fair Commissioner," MSS, WPA biographical file 1428, Wyoming State Archives, 16 August 1938.

Anderson, Nancy F., ed. *Lora Webb Nichols: Homesteader's Daughter, Miner's Bride.* Caldwell, Ida.: The Caxton Printers, Ltd., 1995.

"'Aunt Mattie' Near 96th Year," *Casper Tribune-Herald,* 20 April 1948.

"Aunt Mattie Relives Memories," *Casper Tribune-Herald,* nd.

Baker, Leighton L. *Jim Baker, The Redheaded Shoshone.* Tavares, Fla.: Golden Lifestyles' Books, 1993.

Baker, Rans and Dan Kinnaman. "Fort Halleck." Presentation at annual trek of the Saratoga Historical and Cultural Association, 12 August 1995.

"Bandits Rob U. P. Train," *Rawlins Daily Times,* 13 August 1977.

Bean, Greg. "Butch Cassidy's Sister Dies with Secret," *Casper Star-Tribune,* 11 May 1980.

Beard, Francis Birkhead, ed. *Wyoming From Territorial Days to Present.* Vol. 3. Chicago: The American Historical Society, Inc., 1933.

Beebe, Ruth. *Reminiscing Along the Sweetwater.* Casper, Wyo.: House of Printing, 1973.

Beeler, Sylvia. "Early Day Wyoming," *The Snake River Press,* 20 July 1978.

Bielak, Peter. "Haggarty Finds Red Iron Ore," *Rawlins Daily Times,* 21 September 1950.

——. "Partners Open Vein of Copper," *Rawlins Daily Times,* 22 September 1950.

——. "Pictures Tell Story of Copper Boom," *Rawlins Daily Times,* 20 September 1950.

"Bill Carlisle Buys Camp Near Laramie," *Saratoga Sun,* 30 September 1937.

Black Diamond, [?] April 1894.

"Boney Earnest, Pioneer of Valley, Passes On," *Saratoga Sun,* 26 October 1933.

Brown, Larry. "Lillian Heath Nelson, Pioneer Woman Doctor," *Wyoming History Journal,* 67, no. 2 (Autumn 1995).

"Butch Cassidy Gave Getaway Horse to 10-Year-Old," *Newsletter of the National Association and Center for Outlaw and Lawman History,* 1, no. 2 (Summer, 1975).

"Butch Cassidy's Death Still Debated," *Casper Star-Tribune,* 31 October 1995.

"Butch Cassidy's Memory Lingers in Carbon County," *Rawlins Daily Times,* 6 August 1983.

Burroughs, John Rolfe. *Where the Old West Stayed Young.* New York: William Morrow and Company, 1962.

Busler, Sherrie. "Sun Family Artifact Collection Makes Welcome Addition to County Museum," *Rawlins Daily Times,* 6 August 1983, Fair Edition.

Carbon County Clerk of District Court, Rawlins, Wyo. Probate file 503, Ella Watson.

Carbon County Journal, 8 November 1879–20 December 1879.

——. 7 February 1880–11 September 1880; 1 April 1882.

Carey, Will Gage. "Joe Rankin's Ride," B-R167-jo, American Heritage Center, University of Wyoming (hereinafter American Heritage Center).

"Carlisle Laughs at Pursuers; Drops Gun for Fancy Work," Bill Carlisle file, Carbon County Museum, Rawlins, Wyo.

"Carlisle Remains A.W.O.L.," *Rawlins Republican,* 27 November 1919.

Carlisle, William L. *Bill Carlisle, Lone Bandit: An Autobiography.* Pasadena, Cal.: Trail's End Publishing Company, Inc., 1946.

Casper Tribune-Herald, 3 June 1949.

———. 21 August 1961.

"Charlie Winter to Start Campaign to Have Forts Set Aside by Government," *The Guernsey Gazette,* 19 February 1926.

Chatterton, Fenimore C. *Yesterday's Wyoming: The Intimate Memoirs of Fenimore C. Chatterton, Territorial Citizen, Governor, Builder.* Denver: Powder River Publishers and Booksellers, 1957.

Clarke, J. J. to I. M. Conness, 22 January 1930, Mexico. Taylor Pennock file, MSS 793, Wyoming State Archives.

"Controversy Over Street Names Recalls Thornburg Battle Story," *Laramie Republican-Boomerang,* 18 January 1928.

"Correspondent Tells Great Story About Tie Camp," *Grand Encampment Herald,* 17 July 1903.

Coutant, C. G. *History of Wyoming From Earliest Known Discoveries.* 3 vols., Laramie, Wyo.: Chaplin, Spafford, and Mathison Printers, 1899.

De Trobriand, Regis Philippe. *Military Life in Dakota.* Translated by Lucille M. Kane. St. Paul: Alvord Memorial Commission, 1951.

Dodge, Richard I. *Our Wild Indians: 33 Years Personal Experience Among the Red Men of the Great West.* Hartford, Conn.: A. D. Worthington and Company, 1883.

"Dr. J. E. Osborne Takes Students Through Egypt," *Rawlins Republican,* 27 November 1928.

"Down the Tramway Comes the Copper," *Grand Encampment Herald,* 9 June 1903.

Denver Post, 21 December 1918, p. 10.

Dunham, Dick. "When the Outlaws gathered for Thanksgiving," *Denver Post Empire Magazine,* 20 November 1977.

Early History of Saratoga and Vicinity, Bicentennial Edition. Compiled by the History Committee. Saratoga Historical and Cultural Association.

"Ed Haggarty Victim of Slight Stroke," *Saratoga Sun,* 14 October 1937.

Ellis, Mrs. Charles. "Carbon County," MSS, WPA Subject 895-#129I, Wyoming State Archives.

Erb, Louise Bruning, Ann Bruning Brown and Gilberta Bruning Hughes. *The Bridger Pass Overland Trail 1862-1869 Through Colorado & Wyoming and Crossroads at the Rawlins-Baggs Stage Road in Wyoming.* Littleton, Colo.: ERBGEM Publishing Company, 1989.

Erhard, George. J. "True Pioneer Tells of Brown's Park in 70s; of Isom Dart and Tom Horn," *Rock Springs Rocket,* 1 March 1929.

———. "Mystery Murders of Matt Rash and Isom Dart Now Believed the Dastardly Acts of Tom Horn," *Rock Springs Rocket,* 5 April 1929.

Ernst, Donna B. "Wanted Friends of the Wild Bunch," *True West*, December 1994.

Evans, Elva. "Margaret Pearson Spends Lifetime in Platte Valley," *Saratoga Sun*, 29 June 1988.

——. "Platte Valley Men Served as County's First Legislators," *Saratoga Sun*, 4 July 1990.

——. "Reflections from our files 100 years ago," *Saratoga Sun*, 13 December 1995.

Fenwick, Robert W. "Lillian Heath, M. D., Wyoming's First Lady of Medicine," *Denver Post Empire Magazine*, 28 August 1955.

"Ferris-Haggarty Discoverer Started Poor," *Rawlins Daily Times*, 14 August 1976.

Finney, Lynn Phillips. Interview by author. Encampment, Wyo., 22 November 1995.

Flanagan, Mike. "Fake pistol opened door to career in crime," *Denver Post*, 4 February 1990.

Frederick, J. V. *Ben Holladay, The Stagecoach King*. Lincoln, Nebr.: University of Nebraska Press, 1940.

"Funeral Held for Pearl Savage," *Saratoga Sun*, 20 December 1979.

Gill, Dr. George. Telephone interview with author, March 1997.

"'Gold in them thar hills' Said Pioneer Prospector," *Saratoga Sun*, 28 April 1932.

Gould, Lewis L. "Francis Warren and the Johnson County War," *Arizona and the West*, 9, no. 2

"Governor Osborne," *Annals of Wyoming*, 12, no. 1, 1940.

Grand Encampment Herald, 22 July 1897–17 October 1901.

Hafen, LeRoy, ed. *The Mountain Men and the Fur Trade of the Far West*. Vol. 3. Glendale, Calif.: The Arthur H. Clark Company, 1966.

Harrell, Ida Purdy. "Sketch on Merritt D. Houghton and Fannie Houghton," MSS, H63-129, Wyoming State Archives.

Harrington, M. C., Maj. D.E.O., U.S.A. Ret. "The Thornburg Massacre," *The Cactus*, December 1929 and January 1930.

Heath, Dr. Lillian. Reel-to-reel taped interview, Helen Hubert Collection Number 1003, Folder 1, January 1961. American Heritage Center. Rawlins, Wyo.

Historic Downtown Rawlins Walking Tour. Carbon County Museum.

"History of Ed Bennett on the Overland Trail," *Saratoga Sun*, 2 April 1903.

History of the Union Pacific Coal Mines 1868-1940. Omaha, Nebr.: Colonial Press.

Homsher, Lola and Mary Lou Pence. *Ghost Towns of Wyoming*. New York: Hastings House, 1956.

Huey, William R. *In Search of Hollywood, Wyoming, 1894–The Silent Years-1929*. Self-published, 1985.

Hufsmith, George W. *The Wyoming Lynching of Cattle Kate, 1889*. Glendo, Wyo.: High Plains Press, 1993.

Hull, Jim. "Isom Dart, Gentle Outlaw," *Early History of Saratoga and Vicinity, No. II.* 4 July 1977. Saratoga Historical and Cultural Association.

"In Memoriam—John Eugene Osborne," files, Carbon County Museum.

"Jim Baker in Town," *Denver Republican*, 8 June 1893.

"Judge Winter Succumbs to Long Illness,"*Casper Tribune-Herald*, 23 April 1948.

Katz, William Loren. *Black People Who Made the Old West.* New York: Crowell Publishing, 1977.

Kelly, Charles. *The Outlaw Trail.* New York: The Devon-Adair Company, 1959.

Kuykendall, W. L. Judge. *Frontier Days: A True Narrative of Striking Events on the Western Frontier.* J. M and H. L. Kuykendall, Publishers, 1917.

Larson, T. A. *History of Wyoming*, 2nd ed., rev. Lincoln, Nebr.: University of Nebraska Press, 1978.

"Leading Hotels in Wyoming," *Cheyenne Daily Leader*, 21 November 1902.

"Letter from North Platte Crossing," *Frontier Index*, 23 June 1868.

Linford, Velma. *Wyoming, Frontier State.* Denver: The Old West Publishing Company, 1947.

MSS 156, handwritten. (About Ed Bennett) Wyoming State Archives.

Martin, Mary and Gene. *Colorado's Hall of Fame: A Quick Picture History*, 1st ed. Colorado Springs, Colo.: Little London Press.

McElroy, John J. "Bonabel's Watch: A Story of the Overland Trail and the North Platte Crossing," WPA Subject 1421, Wyoming State Archives.

McLaird, James. Telephone interview with author, April 1999.

McMahan, Kristina E. "Violence on the Frontier: Case Study Big Nose George Parrott." Masters thesis, University of Wyoming, 1996.

Meadows, Anne and Daniel Buck. "The Last Days of Butch and Sundance," *Wild West*, February 1997.

Meschter, Daniel Y. Collection, Box 3, Abstract of Docket Journal and Testimony. (George Parrott). American Heritage Center.

Miller, Lael. "Mrs. Lou Nelson, Resident 77 Years, Was Early-Day Physician in Rawlins," *Rawlins Daily Times*, 16 August 1955.

Miller, Dr. Mark. "Fort Fred Steele." Presentation to annual trek of Saratoga Historical and Cultural Association. 1994.

———. *Hollow Victory: The White River Expedition of 1879 and the Battle of Milk Creek.* Niwot, Colo.: University Press of Colorado, 1997.

Miniclier, Kit. "Saving the Sun*," Denver Post Magazine*, 28 May 1995.

Morehead, Katherine. "Trapper Left Name on Peak," *Casper Star-Tribune*, 2 January 1976.

Moulton, Candy. "Railroad buff recalls history of S&E," *Saratoga Sun*, 15 April 1982.

———. "An Encampment Duo Wrote the State Song," *Laramie Daily Boomerang*, 10 July 1987.

——. "Ranch Artist," *Wyoming Horizons*, 1 May 1983.

——. "Pen and Ink Artist Records Valley Activity," *Saratoga Sun*, 23 November 1976.

——. "The Big Encampment Smelter," *Laramie Daily Boomerang*, 10 July 1987.

——. *The Grand Encampment*. Glendo, Wyo.: High Plains Press, 1997

——. "The Lingering Legend of Tom Horn," *American Cowboy*. July/August 1995.

——. "The Sun Family: A Colorful Role in Early History," *Rawlins Daily Times*, 28 March 1986. Pioneer Section.

——. "The Man Behind the Grand Encampment Copper Boom," *Rawlins Daily Times*, 8 August 1987. Fair Edition.

——. "Federal Land Concerns Prompt Decision: Three on Sun Ranch to Swap Land," *Wyoming Livestock Roundup*, 31 August 1996.

"Mountains Are Renamed After Pioneers of Valley," *Saratoga Sun*, 6 December 1928.

Mumey, Nolie, *The Life of Jim Baker 1818-1898, Trapper, Scout, Guide, and Indian Fighter*. Denver: The World Press, Inc., 1931.

"Mystery Explained—Old Timer Explains the Mystery of John Henry at Meeteetse," *Basin Republican*, [1911?]

Nichols, Lora Webb. "I Remember: A Girl's Eye View of Early Days in the Rocky Mountains," Grand Encampment Museum, Encampment, Wyo., Typewritten.

"Noted Wyoming Pioneer dies at the age of 80, (n.p., n.d.), W. L. Kuykendall file, Wyoming State Archives.

Nye, Bill. *Forty Liars and Other Lies*. Chicago, Ill.: Bedford and Clarke and Co., 1882.

"Old Carbon County Man is One of Two Oldest Scouts," *Rawlins Republican*, 29 November 1927.

"Oldest Citizen Enters His Protest to Changing Name from Thornburg to Ivinson," *The Wyoming Eagle*, 13 January 1928.

Oldman,Vera. Interview by author. Grand Encampment Museum, Encampment, Wyo., December 1995.

Olson, Kenny. Interview by author. Saratoga, Wyo., December 1995.

Osborne, John E., letter to J.C. Gale, 12 September 1928, Rawlins, Wyo. Union Pacific Historical Museum, Big Nose George file, 201-208.

"Output from Wyoming May Relieve Threatened Copper Famine,"*Grand Encampment Herald*, 30 May 1906.

Owen, W. O. "Jo Rankin's Great Ride: The Ute Uprising of 1879, The Meeker Massacre," B-R167-jo, American Heritage Center.

——. "Armed Sentries Once Guarded a Dance at Saratoga," WPA file 950, Wyoming State Archives.

Pennock, Taylor to Mrs. Cyrus Beard, 3 April 1930, Saratoga, Wyo. Taylor Pennock file, MSS 715, Wyoming State Archives.

Perue, R. Richard. Interview by author. Saratoga, Wyo., 1 December 1995.

Post, Marie Caroline de Trobriand. *The Life and Memoirs of General de Trobriand, U.S.A.* New York: E. P. Dutton & Company, 1910.

Progressive men of the State of Wyoming, no author listed, Chicago: A.W. Bowen and Company, 1903.

Provorse, Jane. "The Ferris Mansion,"*Wyoming Horizons*, 2 October 1983.

Rankin, Joe. File H56-52, scrapbook of newspaper clippings. Wyoming State Archives.

———. MSS 86, Wyoming State Archives.

———. to Attorney General of the United States, 31 October 1892, File H88-33, Wyoming State Archives.

Rankin, M. Wilson. "Reminiscences of Frontier Days," Diary of M. Wilson Rankin, 978R211, film H-190-H-191. Wyoming State Archives.

Rawlins Daily Times, 12 May 1950.

"Recollections of Taylor Pennock,"dictated to I. R. Conniss, *Annals of Wyoming*, 6 no. 1 and 2, July/October, 1929.

Reed, Chuck. Telephone interview with author, 13 November 1995.

"Richard Savage, Carbon County Pioneer, is 98," *Rawlins Republican*, 5 July 1939.

Rivera, Rubie. "Memories," 1925, Carbon County Museum, Rawlins, Wyo., typewritten.

———. "Things Worth While I Can Remember During My Life, Both in California and Wyoming," 1925, Carbon County Museum, Rawlins, Wyo., typewritten.

Roybal, Rose. "Boney Earnest, One of Oldest Old Timers Writes from Alcova," 1939, WPA Subject 1413, Wyoming State Archives.

———. "Resident of Rawlins for Over 50 Years Dies in Denver," 7 September 1938. WPA biographical files 820 and 1800, (Rubie Rivera), Wyoming State Archives.

Sackett, —. "Boney Earnest, Bullwhacker," WPA biographical file 295, Wyoming State Archives, n. d.

Saratoga and Encampment, Wyoming: An Album of Family Histories. A Wyoming Centennial Lasting Legacy Project by the Joint Centennial Committee of Saratoga and Encampment, Wyo. The Woodlands, Texas: Portfolio Publishing Company, 1989.

"Scientists Reconstructing Legend of Big Nose George,"*Rawlins Daily Times*, 1 November 1995.

Sielaff, Jane. Interview by author. Little Snake River Museum, Savery, Wyo., Summer 1995.

"Sister Says Butch Cassidy 'Got Off on Wrong Foot'," *The Wyoming Eagle*, 12 June 1974.

Sprague, Marshall. "Hero on Horseback," *Denver Post Empire Magazine*, 16 June 1957.

———. "Massacre: The Tragedy at White River," Boston: Little, Brown and Co., 1957.

Spring, Agnes Wright. "First Sheep Wagon Was Evolved and Built by Rawlins Blacksmith Fifty-Six Years Ago," *Saratoga Sun*, 12 December 1940.

———. *Rawlins Republican-Bulletin*, 2 May 1939. Union Pacific Old Timers Edition.

"Stage Upset on a Curve," *Denver Post*, 26 October 1898.

Steele, John. *Across the Plains in 1850*. Chicago: Printed for the Caxton Club, 1930.

Stiff, Cary. "Isom Dart: The Rustler Who Tried to Go Straight," *Denver Post*, 13 July 1969.

"Story of 'Joe Rankin's Record Run' is Told in Address by C. P. Arnold," *Rawlins Republican*, 24 September 1929.

"Strung Up; The True Story of the Lynching of Jas. Averell and Ella Watson," *Carbon County Journal*, 27 July 1889.

Sun, Kathleen. Interview by author. Rawlins, Wyo., 27 September 1995.

Swisher, T. J. Dr. "Globe Circling Party is Still Following Old Sol on His Nonstop Journey," *Rawlins Republican*, 13 May 1926 and 20 May 1926.

"Taylor Pennock, Pioneer of the Valley, Died Tuesday," *Saratoga Sun*, 16 June 1932.

"Teachers in Session," *Laramie Republican*, 5 September, [1895?]

"The Copper King of Wyoming," *Cheyenne Daily Leader*, 6 August 1900.

"The Hanging—the Graphic Account of Eye Witnesses," *Carbon County Journal*, 3 August 1889.

"The Meeker Massacre," *Annals of Wyoming* 16, no.2.

"The Stagecoach King of the West Operated from Missouri", *Missouri Historical Review*, July 1954.

"The Thornburgh Battle with the Utes on Milk Creek," *The Colorado Magazine*, 13, no. 3, May 1936.

Thompson, John Charles. "Alleged Son of Cattle Kate Paints Virtuous Picture of Lynching Victim," *Wyoming State Journal*, 28 March 1940.

———. "In Old Wyoming," B-K969-wL, American Heritage Center.

"Thousands Hear Congressman Winter Talk About State," *Casper-Herald*, 25 April 1925.

"Tom Sun Came to State After Civil War,"*Republican-Bulletin*, 2 May 1939.

"Tom Sun Founded an Enduring Legacy," *Rawlins Daily Times*, 6 August 1983. Fair Edition.

Turchen, Lesta V. and James D. McLaird. *The Black Hills Expedition of 1875*. Mitchell, S.Dak.: Wesleyan University Press, 1975.

U. S. Army, Office of the Adjutant General. *Official Army Register for 1895*. Washington, D.C. 1 December 1894.

———. *Official Army Register for 1896*. Washington, D.C., 1 December 1895.

U. S. Department of the Interior, National Park Service and Wyoming Recreation Commission, *National Register of Historic Places Inventory—Nomination Form*, 1972. (Junge, Mark. "The Grand Encampment," adapted.)

"Ute Massacre," *The Cheyenne Daily Leader*, 3 October 1879.

Van Pelt, Lori. "The Savage House: Framework of a Romance," *The Fence Post*, 9 January 1995.

———. "Hotel Wolf celebrating 100 years," *Saratoga Sun,* 29 December 1993. Special Section.

———. "Several owners imprint style on Hotel," *Saratoga Sun,* 29 December 1993. Special Section.

Verplanke, April. "Communities Linked by Early Newswomen," *Rawlins Daily Times,* 9 June 1984. Saratoga Centennial Edition

Vyvey, Candy. "Emerson Shows an Interest, Town Booms," *Saratoga Sun,* 29 July 1976.

Walck, E. W. Sr. Interviews by author. Saratoga, Wyo. Various dates.

Watson v. A. J. Bothwell and John Durbin, 458, Carbon County Clerk of District Court, Rawlins, Wyo.(1889).

Webb, Frances Sealy. "Tom Sun Ranch on the Sweetwater is historic," *Casper Tribune-Herald.* n.d. Annual Wyoming edition.

"White Masked Bandit Surrenders When Murder is His Last Chance," *Denver Post,* 23 April 1916.

"'Wild Bunch' Cassidy's Gang," *Rawlins Daily Times,* 13 August 1977.

Willford, Maude Wenonah. *Over the Hills and Prairies of Wyoming: Stories and Poems of the West by a Pioneer.* Denver, Colo.: Big Mountain Press, 1963.

Winter, Charles E. Honorable. "Wyoming, a Sovereign State's Institutions, Peoples and Resources," speech given in U. S. House of Representatives, 22 March 1928. United States Government Printing Office, Washington.

Winter, Charles E. and Earle R. Clemens. *Wyoming, The Wyoming State Song.* Grand Encampment, Wyo: The Herald Publishing Company, 1903.

"Winter Asks Equal Justice for Public Land States,"*Inland Oil Index,* 1 October 1926.

"Winter Writes Book on Land Question," [Newspaper clippings, assorted]. 1932. Wyoming State Archives.

Wright, Kathryn, "Dad Rode with the Wild Bunch," *True West,* January/February 1979.

"Wyoming's Pioneer Woman Doctor Visits Hospitals Here After 36-Year Retirement," *Denver Post,* 30 August 1955.

Index

About the Author

Lori Van Pelt's articles have appeared in a variety of regional and national magazines including *Persimmon Hill, Art of the West, Old West, The Fence Post,* and *Western Horseman.* A former staff writer for the *Saratoga Sun,* her work has also appeared in various Wyoming newspapers. Her professional memberships include Western Writers of America, Women Writing the West, and Wyoming Writers, Inc., in which she currently serves as Vice President. She has recently completed a historical novel and is currently at work on a historical biography and a collection of essays. She and her husband, Eugene Walck, Jr., live on the family ranch near Saratoga, Wyoming.

A special limited cloth edition
of 200 copies of this volume
was printed simultaneously with the trade paperback edition.
The special edition is Smythe sewn, bound in juniper Roxite B cloth,
and stamped in copper foil.
It is designed to be sold without a dust jacket.

The text is composed in
eleven point Adobe Garamond.
Display type is Post Antiqua by Adobe
with ornaments from Border Dingbats.
The book is printed on sixty pound Thor
acid-free, recycled paper
by Thomson-Shore.